PLACES AND NAMES

ALSO BY ELLIOT ACKERMAN

Waiting for Eden

Dark at the Crossing

Green on Blue

PLACES AND NAMES

ON WAR, REVOLUTION,
AND RETURNING

Elliot Ackerman

PENGUIN PRESS
NEW YORK
2019

PENGUIN PRESS
An imprint of Penguin Random House LLC
penguinrandomhouse.com

LIBRARY OF CONGRESS CATALOGING-IN-PUBLICATION DATA
Names: Ackerman, Elliot, author.
Title: Places and Names : Reflections on War, Revolution,
and Returning / Elliot Ackerman.
Description: New York, New York : Penguin Press, [2019]
Identifiers: LCCN 2018041429 (print) | LCCN 2018042703 (ebook) |
ISBN 9780525559979 (ebook) | ISBN 9780525559962 (hardcover)
Subjects: LCSH: Ackerman, Elliot. | Iraq War, 2003–2011--Biography. |
United States. Marine Corps--Officers--Biography.
Classification: LCC DS79.766.A25 (ebook) | LCC DS79.766.A25 A3 2019 (print) |
DDC 956.7044/34092 [B]--dc23
LC record available at https://lccn.loc.gov/2018041429

Printed in the United States of America
1   3   5   7   9   10   8   6   4   2

Book design by Daniel Lagin

For Chui

In the story of Patroclus

no one survives, not even Achilles

who was nearly a god.

Patroclus resembled him; they wore

the same armor.

Always in these friendships

one serves the other, one is less than the other:

the hierarchy

is always apparent, though the legends

cannot be trusted—

their source is the survivor,

the one who has been abandoned.

What were the Greek ships on fire

compared to this loss?

In his tent, Achilles

grieved with his whole being

and the gods saw

he was a man already dead, a victim

of the part that loved,

the part that was mortal.

—"The Triumph of Achilles," Louise Glück

Contents

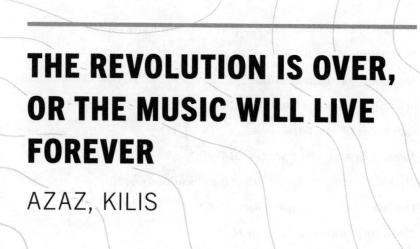

THE REVOLUTION IS OVER, OR THE MUSIC WILL LIVE FOREVER

AZAZ, KILIS

Prologue

Crowds in the streets, marches, songs. Those are finished now. The revolution is over. The war can begin. A column of smoke boils upward from Azaz, a hamlet along Syria's northern border with Turkey. Beneath a blanket of slate clouds, the *whip-crack* of rifle fire comes at odd intervals: the Islamic State battles the Northern Storm, a brigade of the dissolving Free Syrian Army. The air is still, no wind. The smoke continues to climb, perfectly straight, building like an obelisk. A monument.

Azaz's sister town is Kilis, a backwater tucked among the mossy low hills of Turkey's southern border. Just after sunrise, a week ago, the journalist Steven Sotloff crossed here; that same afternoon he disappeared on the road to Aleppo. A year later the Islamic State will behead him. Today that group's name means nothing. They are virtually unknown. Today a revolution is ending.

All I know is I have come to be close to something familiar. Standing along the roadside in Kilis, just next to the border crossing, everything is confusion, confusion and suitcases. The morning's refugees don't know what to do with themselves, so they move their suitcases from one side of the road to the other. They stack them by the bus stop, a single bench beneath an overhang, a schedule tacked to its side. They read the schedule; it has no meaning—the buses don't come. They glance at their watches, checking the time, which also has no meaning—the hour and minute hands will never point out the answer of how long they must wait. A column of halted sixteen-wheelers also waits, stalled at the border. The cargo can go no further, but it can't go back. Confusion is suitcases. Confusion is halted sixteen-wheelers. Confusion is waiting.

———

Farther from the road, where the morning's refugees have yet to venture, there is a camp. Behind a chain-link fence, tents are neatly aligned, and between their rows children play simple games—hide-and-seek, hopscotch, tag—and women watch. The men pass quickly from one tent to another, staring at the ground, hiding their faces as if hiding all they've lost. Outside the camp's entrance, a steel revolving door the same as a subway turnstile, an entrepreneurial Turk has built a café. It is simple: plastic chairs and tables, a propane stove for tea, a refrigerator for bottled water and soda, some packaged foods—potato chips and chocolates.

My companion on this trip, and for many months to follow, is Matt, a friend of a friend, who has spent the last six years living in northern Iraq and in downtown Kabul, teaching at the American university in both places. At the café, he orders a pot of tea and a plate of refreshments. Matt's purpose at the border is more practical than mine—he wants to see if it is open. Only the week before, he incorporated the Syrian Research and Evaluation Organization, or SREO, or as he says it, *sur-rey-oh*, a start-up that will bid on contracts from international organizations, auditing their humanitarian relief programs or subcontracting their excess work. A boom of aid has flooded into this conflict, and that parallel economy gives Matt his ticket to ride.

One at a time, a cluster of men gathers around Matt, who comes to his feet, offering his hand and stopping the conversation to welcome each who joins this group. Matt rowed heavyweight crew at Boston University. His arms are enormous. No one stands taller than his chin, which is covered with a full, blond beard. His eyes are blue. When I come over, no one stands. I sit among the refugees and Matt. Our conversation is in Arabic, Turkish, broken English. We wrestle with language as we wrestle with our topic: Why would two rebel groups—the Islamic State and the Free Syrian Army—fight one another? Wasn't the revolution about toppling President Bashar al-Assad? What is happening in Azaz? What has happened?

The revolution is over. The war is beginning.

The men tell us what we already know, about the fighting, about the politics. We stare at them, as if we might read their histories—the ones we want to understand, the ones they won't likely share—in their faces, which express themselves mainly with anger, sadness, and occasionally humor when explaining some misfortune that pierces the frontier between tragedy and comedy. We watch so closely that we don't drink our tea and we don't eat our food. And when they all stand we are startled. Our eyes follow theirs, and we see someone stumbling toward us.

He is young, in his twenties, and he walks like a man in need of a cane. He wears a black parka that is too heavy for an autumn day. His cheeks are hollow, his complexion tinged a poisonous green, a film of sickness trapped beneath his skin. His gaze rests on our group. He comes closer. His eyes fix on Matt's, shifting to mine. They are blood-shot, a starburst of veins. The group moves aside, allowing him to step in front of us, the pair of Americans. He unzips his parka. Lifting his T-shirt, he winces at the pain. From sternum to waistband he has been flayed open. His scar runs straight as a rail track, and the holes of heavy, unthreaded stitches appear industrial, binding like steel ties. We'd searched the expressions of these other men for some knowledge of this place, one beyond politics and the meaningless movements of armies, but this young man with the serrated scar wears such knowl-edge across his stomach, so much so that what I might learn from his words seems incidental compared with what I might learn from look-ing at his body.

He pins his shirt up with his chin, tracing the length of his scar with the nubs of his index fingers, both of which have been snipped off. He is from Aleppo. He worked in a sugar refinery that was bombed during a regime offensive. This explains the scar. His amputated fingers re-main a mystery. His six-year-old daughter was killed in the same of-fensive, at home with her mother. But he doesn't tell me this—another man whispers it in my ear. Unconscious after the bombing, he was taken to a hospital, which, once the regime advanced, fell into their ter-ritory. Flitting in and out of consciousness, he waited in the hospital for a surgeon, or death. For days he waited. There was a counteroffensive. "Then the Daesh took the hospital," he says. Incomprehension must read across my face, because a man, the same one who explained about his dead daughter and wife, points across the border, to the smoke, and he explains that *Daesh* is the Arabic enunciation of the acronym ISIS, *al-Dawla al-Islamiya al-Iraq al-Sham.* "Because I was in a hospital held by the regime," continues the man with missing fingers, "the Daesh assumed that I supported Assad. They believe that to pray to Mecca one needs fingers to point the way. If the soul wanders, they disfigure the body, as they believe the soul has already been disfigured, removing the index fingers so you cannot pray." What miracle has brought him here, enabling his escape to the relative safety of this place? Matt asks, but no answer is given, and the man pulls down his T-shirt. It is purple with bold yellow letters printed across it, a proclamation in English: "The Music Will Live Forever."

Some Gauloises are set on the table, and everyone takes from the same pack. The Syrians smoke aggressively, lighting one after another, as if by smoking their lives away they exercise some control over them. The conversation returns to the war's strategy, the ever-shifting front lines, the seasons of offensive and counteroffensive. Matt scribbles in a notebook, alternating his stare between the pages, the men, and the distant border. Matt hadn't fought in Iraq and Afghanistan as I had, but we've been affected in much the same way, as evidenced by the fact we've journeyed here, for a litany of reasons, but none greater than to take a look at another war. What we see across the border, in Azaz, is familiar enough, an urban battle waged in this part of the world, but we watch in a different context—this isn't our war. The looks we take seem to be looks back—as if, watching the fight ahead of us, we might understand the one behind us, the violence we'd witnessed in the last decade.

Our conversation is interrupted when the steel turnstile from the camp clangs open. Another man, blond-haired and blue-eyed as Matt, strides toward us. His complexion is ruddy, his fair skin burnt a bright-even red from time in the sun. His camouflage army pants are of a Russian pattern, and holstered to his leg is a medical kit. Everyone stands, even the man with the scar, though he again grimaces at the pain. So Matt and I stand too. With an Eastern European accent, this doctor speaks Arabic. The man with the scar embraces him, the two touching temples together, an intimate sign of friendship. The doctor peels back the purple T-shirt, seeming to examine his recent work. We have been asking questions, but these Syrians look to the doctor as though he has answers. Another chair is brought over. The doctor once again glances at us, the pair of Americans. He works in the camp that we are just visiting—and in his look it seems as though he'd linger for some tea were it not for us. We excuse ourselves and wander toward the border checkpoint to speak with the Turkish gendarmes.

———

Next week, SREO opens for business. Matt's hired a small staff of linguists and researchers—Americans, Canadians, Turks, Syrians—all of whom will live in a single villa in Gaziantep, a Turkish industrial city only a thirty-minute drive from this border crossing in Kilis. I will keep a room in the villa's garret. Living in such proximity to the research staff, I will form close friendships with many of them, but one in particular: Abed, a Damascene activist from the revolution's early days. The two of us will stay up late on the veranda, me smoking cigarettes, mulling over my failed wars, him sipping chai, mulling over his failed revolution. I will learn that the two of us—a former Marine and a former activist—are in many ways veterans of the same conflict, one in which democratic and high-minded ideals have bogged down in the quagmire of Islamist dogma and sectarian bloodshed. Understanding our commonality, we reckon with the destruction our causes left in their wake and consider how to move on from the wreckage of our experience.

Matt and I are walking toward the gendarmes at the border crossing. The tower of smoke climbs ever higher in front of us. We press our American passports to the plexiglass window of the guard booth. The gendarmes fasten their blue tunics. They come to the intercom. Due to the fighting, the border is closed. That morning I make a crossing nonetheless, embarking on a journey to understand the end of a revolution, the beginning of a war. Staring past the gates, past the concertina wire and then farther up the road, what I see is Syria. What doggedly looks back is the last decade in Iraq and Afghanistan: a reflection.

THE TRIUMPH OF DEATH

GHOUTA, MADRID, WASHINGTON, D.C.

y the revolution's second summer, an ever-strengthening chorus of voices calls for the West to intervene. That spring, when
Senator John McCain slips across the border to visit Azaz, he
meets with rebel commanders, to include General Salim Idris, the
leader of the Supreme Military Council of the Free Syrian Army.
"We need American help," Idris tells the press. "We are now in a very
critical situation." When the topic of Russian intervention comes up,
McCain says, "I've been known to be an optimist . . . [but] the reality is
that Putin will only abandon Assad when he thinks that Assad is losing. Right now, at worst it's a stalemate. In the view of some, he is winning."

"What do you think?" I ask Mike, a friend of mine and used-to-be
Marine infantryman. We're at a bar in Georgetown, it's midsummer,
and our faces are upturned to the television, which plays on mute, a
ticker of closed captions running across the bottom of the screen. A
news anchor shuffles his notes and stares into a distant teleprompter,
asking curt questions so he might get to the next segment.

"If we send the First Marine Division into Syria," Mike says, "I feel
like I should put on my fatigue shirt with my medals and march on the
Capitol, John Kerry style." Mike fought in Afghanistan's volatile Hel-

mand Province. He now owns a coffee shop. "On the other hand," he says, "someone's got to stop what's going on over there." We continue to watch, sitting quietly for minutes at a time as we read the text on the split screen divided between pundits who argue *for* or *against* an intervention on behalf of the rebels. As we read, our silent mouths form the words of their arguments as if we are holding a debate with ourselves. Thus far, the great democracies of the West have adopted a policy of "wait and see," perhaps better described as "see and wait": the West is watching, biding its time and hoping that Assad will topple along with his regime. He doesn't. For years, he's hung on.

Then Ghouta, and it seems the waiting will end.

⸻

At 2:00 a.m. on August 21, 2013, the weather at Damascus International Airport is clear, 23°C, with 69% humidity. A breeze blows at 11.1 kilometers per hour (6.9 mph) from the west-southwest. By 5:00 a.m., seven rockets, each containing two liters of sarin nerve agent, land in Ghouta, a rebel-held suburb of Damascus, and the temperature drops to 21°C. Then humidity increases to 83%, and the wind increases to a moderate breeze of 22.2 kilometers per hour (13.8 mph) from the southwest. The conditions are ideal: the sarin spreads. There is a full moon, which sets twelve minutes after the sun rises at exactly 6:00 a.m., when the light becomes adequate for hundreds of bodies to be videoed in the streets.

⸻

A painting hangs in the Prado. I saw it as a boy. It is a panorama by the sixteenth-century Dutch master Pieter Bruegel the Elder: *The Triumph of Death*. Beneath a smoke-blackened sky, an army of skeletons pillages the land. In the foreground, an armored king felled by an arrow is disrobed by one skeleton while another plunders a barrel of his gold coins. A pair of skeletons ascends a tower, where they gleefully ring a bell signaling the end of days. Everywhere the ranks of the dead advance upon the living, who either fly in terror or fruitlessly try to fight back. Those who do fight back turn into a harvest of dead themselves, loaded on wagons to augment the skeleton army's ranks. A ravenous dog gnaws at the face of a child. A clergyman is pushed to the edge of a precipice, helped to his fate by a skeleton who mockingly wears his scarlet cap. A dinner of nobles is broken up. With drawn swords they make a futile resistance. We see the remnants of their meal on the table, a few pallid rolls and, strangely, a severed skull. Mockingly, another skeleton brings them a dish of human bones to feast upon while yet another cinches his arms around a noblewoman's waist, miming the sensuous effects of the dinner party's wine, which has spilled across the table. Fires rage atop a distant hill, which leads to a sea whose shallows are awash with shipwrecks. Barren trees picket a land that is otherwise void of growth. Fish are putrefying on a shore strewn with bloated corpses. The earth is transformed into a blackened cinder, every corner of the landscape stripped of life.

Peasants to nobles, all are taken indiscriminately by death.

Standing in the Prado as a boy, I could not comprehend Bruegel's vision. I remember the confusion I felt, and I recognize the same incomprehension expressed on the dead faces of the children in Ghouta.

Video of the victims creates an international outcry: the British, the Canadians, the Germans, and dozens of other countries condemn the attacks. French president François Hollande proclaims, "France is ready to punish those who took the heinous decision to gas innocents." German foreign minister Guido Westerwelle says, "Germany will be among those that consider it right for there to be consequences." After two summers of fighting, it seems the West will intervene against the Assad regime. Ghouta has created an opportunity for action. An international flotilla of warships is dispatched to the Mediterranean and Red Seas, positioned to strike. The beleaguered Free Syrian Army, long the West's best hope for establishing a democratic and secular new Syria, redoubles its calls for support: We need weapons, we need money, we need the military might of the great democracies. This is the moment. The rebel's champions must take up their cause.

Soon there are questions: Why would Assad launch the sarin? Surely he knows a chemical attack will elicit a response from the West; there are other, less objectionable ways for him to kill a few hundred of his citizens, and President Obama has long been clear about his *red line*. The American public remembers its last war fought on the pretense of *weapons of mass destruction*. Domestic support for a military response is tenuous. Could the rebels, desperate and fatigued from two years of fighting, have engineered this attack to force an intervention? And who are the rebels? Reports circulate that their ranks have become riddled with foreign jihadists: Jabhat al-Nusra, Ahrar al-Sham, Liwa Ahrar

Souriya. We know so little about these groups. If we arm the revolutionaries, will we arm the jihadists as well?

The warships are poised. A hundred Tomahawk cruise missiles have been assigned targets inside Syria, their trajectories set. Then days pass. A debate.

On the pages of major newspapers, these questions are asked. The legislative chambers of the Western powers are scheduled to convene. Intelligence agencies spill out fragmented reports: no one has an answer, no one knows. So few have traveled there. After Ghouta, the voices demanding action are at their strongest yet: *The Islamists hold little sway. We can work with the moderate rebels. The revolution isn't over. The revolution can be won.*

But support crumbles abroad. British prime minister David Cameron holds a vote in Parliament, a motion to intervene in Syria: it is struck down. French president François Hollande's ministerial cabinet presents him with successive polls showing nearly 70 percent of his people are against an intervention: he won't commit without broader international support. President Obama's allies fall away. Ten days after the attack in Ghouta, he stands alone in the Rose Garden, flocked by the White House press corps. Though he has the authority to act, he announces he will take the matter of intervention to a Congress known for indecision: "While I believe I have the authority to carry out this military action without specific congressional authorization, I know that the country will be stronger if we take this course, and our actions will be even more effective."

The same weekend as President Obama's remarks, editorials for or against intervention run in the press alongside maps of Syria with the positions of moderate rebels and Islamists drawn out in straight lines, which are as neat and understandable as the borders created by Sykes-Picot, the treaty which drew the modern Middle East after the First World War. Monday is Labor Day; on Tuesday the Senate convenes. Along an oak dais, thick like a barricade, perch members of the Foreign Relations Committee. The arguments begin.

Present in the chamber are two iconic veterans of America's war in Vietnam: Secretary of State John Kerry and Senator John McCain. Kerry sits beneath the senators, at a conference table. He knows this chamber well, having served here for twenty-eight years. He first came not as a senator but as a witness, to testify. He was twenty-seven years old then. He wore the shirt from his military fatigues, his thick pompadour combed to the side, his many commendations for valor pinned to his chest, speaking out against US policy in Vietnam. "How do you ask a man to be the last man to die for a mistake?" he had said.

Kerry finishes his opening remarks, making the case for an intervention against the Assad regime. A shrill cry erupts behind him, a protestor from the liberal activist group Code Pink: "The American people do not want this! We don't want another war!" A gavel drops and drops again as pleas for order roll across the floor. Then Kerry interjects: "The first time I spoke before this committee . . . I had feelings very similar to that protestor, and that is why it is so important we're all here, having this debate, talking about these things before the country." The senators cycle through their questions. They challenge Kerry on whether the United States will eventually commit ground troops, on whether a limited strike against Assad might further entrench him, on whether America's interests even extend to Syria.

Then it is McCain's turn: "Over the weekend the *Wall Street Journal* ran an important op-ed. . . . I hope you saw it." He begins to read, summarizing its arguments, which fall in a quick succession across the chamber: *the resistance in Syria is not dominated by Islamist die-hards, the Free Syrian Army continues to lead the fight against the regime, they've demonstrated a willingness to submit to civilian authority.* McCain has famously seen the worst of war, held captive in a North Vietnamese prison camp for five and a half years, his legs broken, his wounds infected. When it comes to matters of peace and war, both he and Kerry speak with credibility.

McCain finishes reading. He looks to Kerry. "John, do you agree?" Kerry nods, and adds, "The fundamentals of Syria are secular and I believe will stay that way." McCain leans over his microphone, cutting off Kerry. "I think it's very important to point out again, as you just said: it's a secular state. They would reject radical Islamists."

After a few hours, the hearing concludes.

A vote is taken.

Senate Joint Resolution 21, Authorization for the Use of Military Force Against the Government of Syria to Respond to Use of Chemical Weapons, passes the Senate.

———

Long before that summer, I would read the headlines coming out of Syria, I would follow the debates around intervention, and I would wonder what might happen. Increasingly, I found myself seeking out friends of mine from the Marines, like Mike, so I could see what they thought about the prospect of another Middle Eastern war. I sought them out like a sad case asking after an old girlfriend, as if I just wanted to know what she was up to, as if I just wanted to suck out that last little bit of marrow from a dead romance. Then I met Matt.

It was the spring before the Ghouta attack, three months before the Senate debate. I was pressed into the D.C. Metro on the ride into work as I commuted to a government job that had once seemed important. My cell phone rang between stations. On the other end was an old family friend, a journalist who'd spent decades reporting on conflicts all over the globe. She spoke quickly, insisting that I meet Matt, who was in town for a couple of nights from Kabul. "You two will become friends," she predicted as my train disappeared into another tunnel and our call lost service.

He sat at a bar in Georgetown, the same one where I'd sat with Mike some weeks before. We talked about Iraq—where he had worked at the American University in Sulaimani—and about Afghanistan— where he currently worked at the American University in Kabul. He had other projects as well, most recently an effort to be the first American to visit with Taliban leaders in the Korengal Valley, also known as the "Valley of Death," which US forces had ceded control of two years before. But he was done with Afghanistan. He was looking to move on.

"To what?" I asked.

"To Syria," he said.

Matt had saved up some money—quite a bit, he explained. "I don't spend much, living in these places," he said. "But I've been paid a lot." While we were on the topic of money, he described how much he had seen wasted by humanitarian aid organizations in both countries performing *needs assessments*, the studies used to allocate resources. "I'm thinking about starting a company in southern Turkey, along the border, that will bid on needs assessments inside of Syria. The place is like a black hole. Nobody really knows what's going on." His idea was simple: by hiring locally, by keeping his workforce lean, he could underbid the bloated aid agencies that were only beginning to work inside Syria.

We talked about Iraq and Afghanistan, swapping stories of places—towns, villages, other valleys of death—intoning the familiar names like spells. Then he asked what I thought of his idea.

The television above the bar was switched to the news. I couldn't help but check the headlines as we spoke. Glancing up at them once more, I told him that if he started his company, I wanted to come—not to work, just to be there. He agreed, not needing to ask why, or at least not asking me to explain.

———

In the days after the Senate vote, Matt and I email constantly. I book my ticket to Gaziantep, where his offices will be based. "It's going to be busy," Matt writes, as we brace for what looks like another US war. The debate then moves from the Senate to the House of Representatives. President Obama has less support here: the Republicans control this chamber. The stakes are high: not only does the future of Syria's moderate opposition hang in the balance, but also the credibility of a presidency that seems unable to garner support for its foreign policy. The Democratic whips maneuver, corralling votes in the House for the president's motion to authorize force against the Assad regime. But the votes aren't there.

The debate is stalling in the House. President Obama can't back down on eliminating Assad's chemical weapons, but he can't proceed with the use of force without congressional support. He is stuck. The rebels are stuck: the Western intervention they've fought the last two years to achieve will melt away unless Congress acts.

It's the Monday after the Senate vote. Secretary Kerry is in London, holding a press conference at the Foreign Office. "Is there anything Assad's government can do to avoid an American attack?" shouts a journalist from the press pool. Kerry clutches the side of the dais, hangs his head, as if exhausted by the question, the debate, his inability to convince. He looks up. "Sure, he could turn over every single bit of his chemical weapons to the international community in the next week." Then Kerry throws his hands in the air. "Turn it over, all of it, without delay. . . . But he isn't about to do it and it can't be done."

Phones start ringing. Russia, Syria's staunch ally and America's old adversary, enters the fray. Foreign Minister Sergey Lavrov, acting on President Vladimir Putin's orders, makes an offer: the Russians will broker the destruction of Assad's chemical weapons as Kerry suggests, negotiating a settlement that will avert war. They will save both the Syrian regime and the Americans from their predicament. What's more, they will defuse the crisis that Ghouta has created. Crisis and opportunity, different words for the same thing: the Russians will eliminate the opposition's opportunity for an intervention by the West. Putin achieves all this in one swift diplomatic coup.

The moment for intervention has passed. The United Nations will take away Assad's chemical weapons so he might continue to use other weapons to kill his people. Then the next year, in 2014, after the Democrats lose the Senate, Senator McCain will become the chairman of the Armed Services Committee, a position of enormous leverage. He will come to press for American support of the Syrian rebels with renewed gusto, perhaps even greater than before, as if he wants to expurgate his loss during the Ghouta debate.

———

A month after Putin's intervention, I am traveling the road between Kilis and Gaziantep with Matt as we return from our first trip to the border. I'd taken some notes that morning, and as I review them, the image of the Syrian man, the serrated scar bisecting his flayed stomach, projects across my mind. And his shirt: "The Music Will Live Forever." I return to that day long before, when I stood in the Prado as a boy. As the army of skeletons ravages the land, none are spared in Bruegel's vision, except for one. In the bottom right corner of the painting, a smiling Death plays music from his lute while in front of him, for his entertainment, an unwitting fool plays along.

THE FOURTH WAR

AKÇAKALE

The night before leaving the villa in Gaziantep, Abed and I had agreed: when I met Abu Hassar, we'd lie and tell him that I had been a journalist.

The week before, Abed had taken a day trip to Akçakale refugee camp to check on conditions for one of SREO's reports. The night he returned, I was washing dishes in the kitchen when he said, "I met a guy I think you should meet."

"Okay," I replied, "who is he?"

"He fought in Iraq for al-Qaeda," answered Abed, "but I think you two would really get along." Intrigued by the prospect, I agreed to return to Akçakale with Abed. But would Abu Hassar want to meet with a former Marine? That's when we decided it'd be best to tell him I had spent my time in Iraq as a journalist, and see how our conversation went.

We drive out of Gaziantep early in the morning. It is November, just above freezing. On the outskirts of town, we pick up a twenty-piece box of baklava—Abu Hassar's favorite, I'm told. Then we take the autobahn, a newly completed feat of Turkish engineering, past the city of Şanlıurfa, toward the refugee camp in Akçakale, which is less than a mile from the border where Syrian artillery rounds occasionally land.

"It's going to make talking about Iraq a bit awkward," I say, looking at Abed as he drives.

As we struggle to break 130 kilometers per hour, our black Peugeot shakes like a space shuttle on reentry. Abed glances at me from behind his thin, wire-rimmed spectacles and shifts his eyes quickly back to the road. "Tell him you covered the war," he says, his Damascene accent mixing with an English one, the result of time spent in London and a job he'd once held in the British Consulate's cultural section.

I know Abed is right. Abu Hassar and I are both veterans of the Iraq War, albeit different sides of that war, and even in the abstract, I feel a connection to him, but the hope that he'll feel the same toward me could prove to be naive, even a bit delusional. Abed has explained to me how from 2005 to 2008, Abu Hassar ran guns and fighters across the Syrian border into al-Anbar Province for al-Qaeda in Mesopotamia, right under the nose of Assad's secret police, the mukhabarat. Then, in 2008, the mukhabarat caught him and threw him in jail for three years. He'd only been released when, in the wake of the revolution begun by democratic activists like Abed, Assad emptied the prisons of jihadists in 2011. Assad had hoped the jihadists would fight against him; a regime under siege by radical Islamists is more likely to garner international support than a regime under siege by democratic activists.

To Assad's credit, it worked. Now many of Abu Hassar's old jihadi friends are members of Jabhat al-Nusra and ISIS, the most hard-line and controversial groups in Syria. And Abed, my friend the democratic activist, isn't an activist anymore. He holds down his day job at SREO, and like me, he occasionally files a news story and calls himself a journalist. Who's to say he isn't? Most major papers have shuttered their international bureaus. They rely on freelancers who, for two hundred dollars and a byline, turn in a thousand-word dispatch—far cheaper than keeping someone on staff.

After two hours, we exit the autobahn onto an old and broken road. Abed slows our Peugeot, dodging potholes, driving carefully in the morning rain. My mind churns over the questions I'll ask Abu Hassar. To settle my thoughts, I look out the window. The road is straight and flat. In the distance are the wet hills of Syria's Ar-Raqqah governorate. Between the hills and us, soggy fires burn the bare cotton stalks of an early winter harvest. Bales are stacked in the fields among clods of wet earth. Flecks of cotton rise in the hot air and make little blazes here and there. They look like fireflies in the day.

One of our windshield wipers has broken. It stutters across the glass. Fortunately, it is the one in front of me, and Abed can still see well enough to drive. He points ahead of us. I lean my head over the gearshift to get a look. Like a dirty lake seen from far off, Akçakale refugee camp sits low and gray in the distance. It takes shape as we approach, its tents hung like pavilions behind a thin barbed-wire fence. The pattern reminds me of an empty egg carton expanding for miles on end. Soon I make out dark figures wandering between the camp and the road's shoulder, where they draw rainwater from a ditch.

We pull over, near a cement blockhouse. I move the box of baklava off the back seat and hold it in my lap. Gaziantep is famous for its baklava, and this batch of twenty was expensive. It even came with its own wood-handled carrying case.

Abu Hassar doesn't own a cell phone, a precautionary habit from his jihadi days, so Abed calls Abu Hassar's brother, Abu Ali, who runs a shop out of the blockhouse in front of us. But Abu Ali isn't picking up, and Abed seems in no hurry to walk inside and start asking after either of the brothers.

In front of us, just beyond our windshield, an old man and woman crouch around a trash fire in the rain. Its flame would barely fill a teacup. Just behind them, a tarp is pulled across a now flooded ditch. This is their home.

The heater in our car blows too strongly. I turn it down and fiddle with the baklava's wooden toggles. Abed redials Abu Hassar's brother. He notices my restless hands and assures me, "He is a good guy and excited to meet you."

I watch the old couple, the woman poking the dying fire, the man turning circles, looking for more trash to burn. Now and then both their eyes wander over to the refugee camp that, for whatever reason, they've been refused admittance to. They seem lost as two orphaned children. For a moment, the idea that Abu Hassar will be a no-show leaves me relieved. I will give this old couple my expensive baklava and go home, my good deed done for the day.

"*Yallah!*"

The Peugeot rocks on its axle. Abu Hassar barrels into the back seat, scaring the crap out of us. He knocks loose the olive-green keffiyeh he wears over his black curls. He tightens the keffiyeh back down and grabs Abed by the shoulders, laughing at how badly he's frightened us.

Abed leans forward, searching between his seat and the gearshift. He's dropped his phone. The two begin to speak quickly and in Arabic. Abed smiles, but it is a tight smile that tells me that Abu Hassar has really shaken him and he's a little pissed off about it.

We pull onto the road. Just a few minutes away, in the town of Akçakale, there is a café where we'll drink some tea, eat our baklava, and talk. From behind the steering wheel, Abed introduces me as a journalist. Abu Hassar nods and takes a small vial of perfume from his Adidas sweatshirt. He dabs some into his thick and well-creased hands. He reaches up to the front seat, takes my hand by the wrist, and rubs the perfume from his palm to mine. "The Prophet says there are three things one must never refuse: a good pillow, good yogurt, and good perfume." Abu Hassar presses the perfume into Abed's palm in the same way. I like the part about the perfume and the pillow. I'm not so keen on the yogurt: a bad experience in western Afghanistan once left me bedridden and on an intravenous Cipro drip for almost a week.

"Abu Ali didn't answer the phone. Is he all right?" asks Abed.

Behind me, Abu Hassar begins to laugh again. "He is fine. I was taking noon prayers just behind his shop when you pulled up. I told him not to answer. I wanted to surprise you."

Abed says nothing.

The car becomes quiet, the silence awkward. I make a little small talk. "Is your whole family in the camp?" I ask Abu Hassar.

Abed translates, his eyes fixed on the road.

"Yes, and yours?"

"Yes," I say. "I mean, they're back home."

I ask more about his family. Does he have children? Two boys and a girl, he tells me. The boys are nine and five. His youngest son was born while he was in prison, a topic I know we'll get to. He doesn't tell me how old his little girl is, the age of a man's daughter being a topic of some sensitivity. He asks about my children. I tell him about my son and daughter.

"You are blessed," he says. "How old?"

I take out my iPhone and show him a picture of Ethan. "He's one and a half," I say, stopping myself from scrolling to the next photo, of my daughter.

"A handsome boy," says Abu Hassar. "He looks nothing like you!"

We laugh, and I am grateful for it. I feel reassured that no band of Islamist thugs is waiting at an impromptu checkpoint to kidnap and smuggle Abed and me across the border to star in our own YouTube video.

Soon we are in Akçakale, a crowded town with a single main road. Along that road are a few cafés. The one we park in front of has an Astroturf lawn and white picket fence. Cold as the day is, the outside seats on the Astroturf are filled. Men laze, drinking tea, smoking Gauloises cigarettes and speaking slushy Arabic. Exiting the car, Abed and Abu Hassar chat as I follow behind, carrying the stupid box of baklava by its wooden toggles. Inside, the café is warm. A large man orders the waiters around in Turkish. He seems to be the owner, and he comes to offer us a seat. As he approaches, I tuck the box of baklava in my coat, not certain if we'll be allowed to bring it inside. Abu Hassar sees what I'm doing. He steps in front of me so the owner won't get a good look at my now bulging coat. Abu Hassar then gives me a nod and a sly grin, seasoned smuggler that he is.

Abed greets the owner in Turkish, requesting a quiet seat. We are taken up a narrow stairway. Here, in the back of the café, there is a picnic table. The owner leaves. Awkwardly, we take our seats, not sure who should go where. I wind up sitting next to Abu Hassar, the two of us on the same bench.

Taking off my coat, I place the baklava on the table. Abed opens the box. As he's about to offer some to Abu Hassar, our waiter comes over. The waiter is young, maybe sixteen. He has long black hair, almost to his shoulders. A wispy goatee frames his mouth. He says nothing about the baklava, but stands at the end of our table, his eyes resting on me, as if I should order.

"Chai," I say.

"Français?" our waiter asks me.

Before I can answer, Abu Hassar interrupts. "*La, Amerikee. Ithnan chai.*"

Abed adds, "*Thalatha chai.*"

A pink tulip sits in a glass of water on the table. Abu Hassar begins to twirl it between his index finger and thumb. Abed fills his mouth with a piece of the baklava. I need to get our conversation going. "Abed's told me about your time in Iraq."

Abu Hassar nods.

"I was there too," I say, and add, "as a journalist."

Abu Hassar holds the tulip up to his nose, still saying nothing.

"I hoped we could talk about the war," I say. Abu Hassar gives me a blank look. I'm not getting anywhere. "There is a story I've always liked. It's one from the First World War. The first Christmas on the Western Front." Immediately I think, *Shit, Christmas stories? Dumb move, Ackerman.* But I go on. "The day of the holiday, it snowed. In the cold, the German and British soldiers climbed out of their trenches at a place called Mons. They met in no-man's-land and spent the day swapping small gifts and playing soccer. This Christmas truce became very famous in the West."

Abu Hassar looks at Abed and says something I can't understand in Arabic but that I assume to be "Is this true?"

Abed shrugs.

"What did they do the next day?" Abu Hassar asks me.

"Went back in their trenches and killed each other for another four years."

Abu Hassar laughs. The waiter returns with our tea. I offer Abu Hassar some of the baklava we've brought him. He smiles and takes a piece. "I don't know how good I'll be for your story," he says.

"The story is our conversation," I tell him. "We talk about our war in Iraq and what's going on in Syria right now."

"I'm not as active in the jihad as I used to be," says Abu Hassar.

"Neither am I," I answer.

Abu Hassar laughs again. Then his face turns serious. "The war we fight in Syria is the worst kind, much worse than Iraq." Abu Hassar holds his slender glass teacup by the tips of his thick fingers. He takes a slurp and turns toward me on the bench, holding my eyes with his. "If you lose your money, you can make a new business. If you lose your love, you can find another. Even if you lose your child, you can go to your wife's bed again. But if you lose your country, what can you do? How can you make another country?"

It seems a strange comment coming from Abu Hassar. His friends, both those who fought with the defunct al-Qaeda in Mesopotamia and those who now fight with Jabhat al-Nusra and ISIS, are dedicated to dissolving the current Syrian state. From it, they've committed to building a caliphate spanning from Iraq through Syria and all the way to the Levant. It seems to me that they are the ones bent on destroying his home as it once was.

He looks at me, waiting for a response.

"Do you mind if I take notes?" It is all I can think to say.

He shrugs and plucks another piece of baklava from the box, considering it in his fingers for a moment. "When I was first in the jihad, I was like a starving man feasting on the action. When I got older, I learned to eat more slowly, to be more patient. Even al-Qaeda's best men became too aggressive in Iraq. When they began to kill Christians and Jews who weren't actively against the jihad, this was a mistake. In the Qur'an it says not to do this. In the Bukhari, it is even written that the Prophet once left his armor in the possession of a Jew so it would be protected!" After making this last point, Abu Hassar grins from ear to ear as though he's said something mildly outrageous. I nod back, but wonder if he'd think it outrageous to be having tea with a half-Jewish once-upon-a-time Marine. "For years, I ate like this with al-Qaeda. Now my stomach hurts." I feel I should say something, but before I can Abu Hassar adds, "Still, as much as my stomach hurts, we won, and your country became mired in the Islamic swamp."

"Bush imagined Iraq as if it were France in the Second World War," I say. "As if the Iraqis were just waiting to be liberated. That's what many Americans thought."

"You were wrong," says Abu Hassar. There is no satisfaction in his voice. He simply states the miscalculation that has defined much of his life, and mine. "I regret none of the war," he continues. "When I fought for al-Qaeda, we sent weapons and fighters from Deir ez-Zor into Iraq. Assad left the roads and border open. In Jordan, in Kuwait, in Turkey, not even a dog could wander into Iraq, but from Deir ez-Zor we went where we wanted. Our job was easy. No one asked about our activities. Fighting in the jihad was my true happiness, but Assad proved a greater enemy to you than me."

Abed translates this last point and smirks a bit, as though there is something tragically sentimental about Abu Hassar's love of jihad. I think Abu Hassar catches on, because he adds, "I trained men to fight in explosives, marksmanship, and hand-to-hand combat. I would send them across the border on their missions. They were like the point of the spear. I was like its handle, directing them in the fight. There is nothing closer than those types of friendships. If you were one of my men and you asked me for the last of my water, I would give it to you. If you asked for the last of my food, it would be yours. And if you asked for my life. . . . It is something that can't be understood."

The smirk on Abed's face disappears as he translates this for me. Then Abed adds in English, "This is also how it was among us activists, in the revolution's early days."

I say nothing. For a moment we sit, three veterans from three different sides of a war that has no end in sight. Not the Syrian Civil War, or the Iraq War, but a larger regional conflict. Amidst all of this, Abu Hassar has hit on a unifying thread between us: friendships born out of conflict, the strongest we've ever known. I think that's why I sought out Abu Hassar: to see if that thread binds two people who've fought against each other. And for the first time, I wonder why Abu Hassar has agreed to meet with me, a so-called journalist he knows nothing about, except that I am an American and have spent some time in Iraq. Maybe he, like me, has become tired of learning the ways we are different. Maybe he wishes to learn some of the ways we are the same.

"I think you can tell him," Abed says softly in English.

"You sure?" I ask.

"I think it would be better."

I agree, and Abed explains to Abu Hassar that I had been a captain in the Marines and had fought in Iraq and Afghanistan. I watch them intently, not understanding their quick Arabic. Abu Hassar begins to slowly nod, and his gaze moves from Abed to me. Then, once Abed is done, he picks up the water that has been set on the table. He pours a full glass in front of him, emptying his bottle. He hands it to me.

"A captain," he says. "So we were both like the handle of the spear."

I nod and drink the last of his water.

"Why did you fight?" Abu Hassar asks. "Did you think the war was a good idea?"

"No," I answer. "I thought it was a bad idea."

"Still you fought?"

"When you are a young man and your country goes to war, you're presented with a choice: you either fight or you don't. And you'll always remember what you chose. I don't regret my choice, but maybe I regret being asked to choose. And you? Why did you fight in Iraq? It wasn't your country."

"This isn't true," says Abu Hassar. "My decision was like yours. I am an Arab and a Muslim. That is my country. America invaded Iraq. As a Muslim man, it was my duty to fight." Abed translates, but as he worked at the British Consulate during the height of the Iraq War, this last bit of logic seems to choke in his throat.

Abu Hassar explains how in 2005 he'd gotten involved with al-Qaeda. Before this, he describes himself as "the type of Muslim who didn't fast or pray." Finding Islam late in life, he wanted to be a holy man, but he felt he needed to catch up. He "thirsted for paradise" and was taught that in God's eyes the straightest road there was jihad. He tells me, "A friend gave me books on Islam to study. He also introduced me to some of the jihadists who were in Deir ez-Zor on their way to Iraq. These men had come from places like Yemen, Saudi Arabia, and even as far as Mauritania. Some of them showed me their passports. Each one was thick with stamps, and each stamp was like some medal of the jihad. Seeing how far they had traveled to fight, I felt blessed. All of it was right there for me. Being from Deir ez-Zor, I was like a man who does no work for his harvest."

Abu Hassar then explains the types of operations he was involved in: ambushes, IEDs, raids on checkpoints. He describes a certain attack, one near al-Qaim, a town in western Iraq where I'd been deployed. Abu Hassar's group of fighters had struck an Iraqi Army checkpoint there. "We dressed in their uniforms and were able to get very close to them before we opened fire. We destroyed the checkpoint and withdrew with none of us getting hurt."

"Sounds like a good mission," I reply.

"Yes, very successful." He grins broadly.

"Fun?"

"Yes, fun."

"We never got to do anything like that," I say. "Being in the Marines, most of our missions involved walking around on patrol, waiting to get blown up by you and your friends. We were almost always on the defense."

"Yes, fighting you, we knew this. It was your nature, but it wasn't ours. Jihadists are as keen for death as Americans are for life. In my first year fighting, many of the men I smuggled across the border never returned. These were educated and good men. Later on, when a doctor or a lawyer would arrive in Deir ez-Zor for jihad, I would tell him, 'For you to fight is a waste. If you are a doctor, tend to the wounded fighters. If you are a lawyer, advise the commanders about sharia law. It is your skills that make you most valuable to the jihad.' But these men were eager for paradise. They rarely listened to me."

For a moment, Abu Hassar becomes quiet. He looks across the room, at something that seems just out of view. Abed waves our waiter over. Without asking either Abu Hassar or me what we want, he orders lunch for the three of us.

"It's not like that with all jihad," I say.

"Like what?" replies Abu Hassar.

"I fought in Afghanistan too. The fighters there weren't as eager for death. They would attack and quickly withdraw back up into the mountains. To them, it always seemed important to fight another day."

Abu Hassar nods. "Those who go to Afghanistan are different. It is more difficult to travel there. For them jihad isn't so much a way to die but a way to live."

"They were better fighters," I say.

Abu Hassar frowns. "Perhaps," he says, "but belief is most important. An imam I knew in Deir ez-Zor used to tell the story of a Jew who once came to his mosque. This man began to film prayers each day. After he did this a few times, the imam said to him, 'You are welcome here, it is a house of God, but what are you filming?' The Jew told him that during early-morning prayers the mosque seemed empty and too large, and during Friday afternoon prayers the mosque seemed full and too small. The imam told him, 'This is always the way of things.' The Jew replied, 'Islam will only become the one message when your mosque is as filled at early-morning prayers as it is at Friday-afternoon prayers.'"

Abu Hassar becomes quiet for a moment. He adds some sugar to his tea, stirring it slowly, holding his tiny metal spoon between his thick fingers. "Faith and strength in our ideology is everything."

"I believe that."

"It doesn't require your belief. It is in front of your face to see. The Prophet predicted all that has passed. Before there could be peace, he predicted this period of great wars and many killings. He even predicted what will stop the killings—"

As Abu Hassar rolls into this Islamist polemic, Abed interrupts his translating, scoffs, then turns to me and says with his perfect British accent, "Killing for peace is like fucking for virginity."

I laugh a little and smile at him. Abu Hassar asks Abed something in Arabic. He replies sharply, translating the same to Abu Hassar, whose face contorts around the idea. I'm worried he might take offense, but to my surprise, Abu Hassar begins to laugh too.

"Who said that?" he asks Abed.

"I don't know. Do you?" Abed asks me.

"John Lennon," I say.

"Who's that?" asks Abu Hassar.

"He's an old dead rock singer," I say. "Older than you even." I point to Abu Hassar's thick black beard, which has gone salt-and-pepper.

"War is enough to make you old," answers Abu Hassar. "Assad put the gray in my beard." Then he points to my sunken cheeks, where a couple of gray whiskers have poked through. "George Bush put the gray in yours."

"My children also put the gray in my beard," I reply.

Abu Hassar nods. "Yes," he says. "It is a funny thing: what you love and what you hate both make you old. And I feel old, but am still just thirty-three."

"I'm also thirty-three," I say.

Abed excuses himself and goes to the restroom out back. Abu Hassar and I sit next to each other on the same side of the table. Without our interpreter the space between us becomes awkward. I open my notebook to a clean page. I begin to draw. First, I sketch out a long, oscillating ribbon running from the top left to the bottom right of the page: the Euphrates. Abu Hassar quickly recognizes this. He takes the pencil from my hand and draws the straight borderline between Iraq and Syria, one that cuts through a tabletop of hardpan desert. Along the border he's made, I write a single name: *al-Qaim*.

Next to that name, Abu Hassar writes, *06.2005*. I nod back and write, *09.2004*. I travel farther down the Euphrates and write another name and another date. Our hands now chase each other's around the map, mimicking the way we'd once chased each other around this country. *Haditha: 07.2004 / 02.2005. Hit: 10.2004 / 11.2006*. On it goes. Only the dates and place names matter. These are a common language to us, one not even Abed can translate. Had I understood Arabic or had Abu Hassar understood English, I don't think we would've spoken. The small log we make on these two notebook pages contains the truth of our experience. Soon we've filled most of the map. Between us one thing is missing: we have many places that overlap, nearly all of them, but we don't have a single date that does. Abu Hassar looks at me for a moment. I think he's noticed this too. Neither of us says, or tries to say, anything about it. But I think we are both grateful, or at least I am. Abed comes back from the restroom. I turn my notebook to a clean page.

Before we can resume our conversation, the waiter brings out a large silver tray with our lunch. He lays down three different types of lamb kebab, two plates of kibbe, flatbread, and salads. Then another server comes behind him, carrying a pitcher of *ayran*, a yogurt drink. He pours this into three ornate chalices that look like Turkish knockoffs of the Wimbledon Cup. The cold *ayran* froths as it is poured. As I look down my nose at it, Abu Hassar says, "Remember the Prophet's wisdom: perfume, a good pillow, and yogurt cannot be refused!" He takes a tremendous sip from his cup, the froth sticking to his mustache. Abed drinks too, but before he does, he looks at me and smiles. I take a drink, knowing I have to, and thinking of Cipro.

We eat with our hands, and Abu Hassar asks, "When were you the most afraid in Iraq?"

His question stops me. I've been asked what was the worst thing I'd seen in Iraq (cats eating people), I've been asked what was the bravest thing I'd seen in Iraq (everything Marines do for wounded Marines), I've even been asked by an elderly society lady if I'd killed anyone in Iraq (if I did, you paid me to), but no one has ever asked me when I was the most afraid. I put down my food. It doesn't take long for me to find the answer.

"Getting lost," I say.

Abu Hassar gives me a confused look; so does Abed.

"As an officer," I explain, "I was always leading patrols. Sometimes we'd be in the middle of nowhere, just our column of Humvees and nothing but desert. Even with a GPS, it was easy to get disoriented in a wadi, or to mistake one trail for another. Getting on the radio, telling everyone to stop and turn around because I was lost—the shame of that was my greatest fear."

Abu Hassar and Abed both give me sympathetic looks, as if they recognize some lost part of me in the way I tell this story now. There are other things I could've told them: the time my platoon got cut off and surrounded in a house in Fallujah, or when a truck of Afghan soldiers was torn apart in front of me by a rocket-propelled grenade—all of this had scared me. But if fear is like a disease, these incidents were the twenty-four-hour flu: quick, unpleasant, but passing. The great fears are chronic, never abating, threatening to wear you down. I'm still afraid of getting lost. You should see the map software in my phone.

"God put this fear into you," says Abu Hassar. "You fought in a country that wasn't yours. You were already lost."

"When were you the most afraid?" I ask him.

Abu Hassar explains how at times he'd helped transport al-Qaeda in Mesopotamia field commanders from the border to Damascus. "Some of these men I knew; most I did not. Their work was dangerous; few survived long. I would receive orders from the border emir, the commander who was responsible for smuggling operations. On one occasion, I was given a minivan to transport six operatives to the busy Sarouja neighborhood of Damascus. When I met these operatives at the border, I didn't speak much with them. They were tired, and spent most of our journey sleeping in the back of the minivan. For security purposes, I was told little about what I was doing. I would drive one leg of the journey, call the border emir, and receive instructions for the next. I drove most of that day and that evening; upon arriving at our destination, I called the border emir. He told me to collect 'the equipment' from the operatives. He wouldn't say more than this. We were parked on a busy street. I went to the back of the van and told these men that I needed to collect whatever equipment they had with them. They looked at each other, uncertain what to do. Then one of them stepped from the minivan and into the crowded street. He began to unbutton his shirt. Beneath it, he wore a suicide vest. A couple of the others stepped out of the van too. They also wore suicide vests and also began to strip off their shirts. Before I could tell them to get back in the van, the six men began to argue about whether or not they should have to give up their vests; these operatives had likely worn them for weeks or even months. For that long, they'd been ready to die."

"Did they give up the vests?" I ask.

"I left them arguing in Sarouja."

"That whole ride from the border, any one of them could've blown himself up and killed you."

Abu Hassar gives me a quick, confused look. "No, that's not what I was afraid of. These were good men."

Now I am the one with the confused look.

"What I was afraid of," says Abu Hassar, "was getting arrested right there. When you fought, you only had to worry about living or dying. I also had to worry about disappearing into the belly of some prison. This was my greatest fear. And like all great fears, it happened."

My great fear never happened: after five deployments, I never once got lost on patrol. But I've since thought about what Abu Hassar said, and coming home from the wars, I've learned there are other ways to get lost.

"What was prison like?" I ask.

Abu Hassar's hands become restless. He plays with a fork on the table. "There isn't too much to tell. I spent three years there, most of it in solitary confinement."

"Why were you arrested? I thought the regime left you alone."

Abu Hassar puts the fork down. "They always did, but at the time I was arrested there was a great controversy in my group. Some of the commanders in Iraq had discovered that the border emir I worked for had been taking money from the regime's mukhabarat. They wanted the border emir killed for this. When I smuggled men to and from Iraq, I received messages from some of these commanders telling me I needed to execute the border emir. I didn't know what to do. Then, one night, before I'd chosen to do anything, the mukhabarat came to my house in Deir ez-Zor and arrested me."

"And your family?" I ask.

"My wife was pregnant. She was left at home with my daughter and son. No one knew where I'd been taken. A few weeks later, my brother finally went to the local police station to ask about me. They beat him with canes. For three years I was like a ghost; I'd disappeared. They moved me from prison to prison: Sednaya, Far' Falastin, Adra—I spent time in each. The war in Iraq was winding down. We jihadists, once useful to the regime, no longer were. We were arrested in greater and greater numbers. Assad wished to improve his reputation internationally. Soon the prisons were filled with men I'd fought alongside. The other prisoners were thieves and rapists, but we jihadists were treated worst of all. We were beaten and electrocuted. Torture was part of our life. Some of us died; others went crazy."

Abu Hassar starts playing with the fork again, pricking his thumb against it.

"How long was your sentence?" I ask.

His forehead knots. "There was no sentence," he answers. "I was only released because of him." He points at Abed. "His revolution freed me."

Abed seems at pains to translate this fact. The jihadists within Syria would never have ascended if it weren't for the initial success of the secular- and democratic-minded revolution. As the revolution gained momentum, Assad opened his prisons, unleashing the jihadists on himself.

Abed looks at Abu Hassar, but speaks to me: "At times, I regret my revolution."

Before I can reply, Abu Hassar begins his story again. "When we were released, the fighters I'd known from the Iraq War did just as Assad wanted. They organized against him. My old friends formed Jabhat al-Nusra and ISIS, but I refused to join."

"Were you tired of fighting?"

"No, it wasn't that. Assad wouldn't release these men without ensuring his informers were in place among them. I knew how that would end for me. I have three children. I won't go back to prison, so I came here."

"And do you miss it—the fighting, the excitement?"

Of all the questions I ask, this is the only one Abu Hassar never answers.

"I have something to ask you," he says, changing the subject. "With all your warplanes, and your aircraft carriers, and tanks, and your laser-guided bombs, with all this—"

I interrupt him. "I think I know your question."

Abu Hassar shakes his head. "With all these things, how is it that you couldn't win in Iraq?"

"The type of war we chose was complicated," I say. "We'd lost before we even started fighting. For us, success meant winning. For you, the insurgents, success meant not losing. Those are two very different things."

Abu Hassar looks at me as if I am trying to take something from him, as if my analysis robs him of some honors of combat. "We defeated you with nothing," he says. "With explosives in plastic jugs on the roadside and old rifles. Imagine if we'd had your tanks or your planes."

"The Afghan insurgents say, 'You Americans have the watches, but we have the time.' It's the same here. That's why you won."

Abu Hassar's face tenses, his eyebrows nearly touching, as if unable to understand what I am talking about: *Watches and time? Who has which?* "Just imagine if we had weapons like yours now. Assad would be dead within a few weeks. If Obama armed the Islamists, he wouldn't have to worry about Putin and Khamenei's games."

Right in his face, I laugh.

"You think it's funny, but it's the truth," says Abu Hassar.

It has often been said that the test of a first-rate intelligence is the ability to hold two opposing ideas in thought at the same time while still retaining the ability to function. Based on that criteria, the way most Syrian jihadists and activists think about the United States makes them some of the most intelligent people I've ever met. Like most in the Arab world, they are deeply suspicious of American interventions in the region—the invasion of Iraq was criminal to them. But held in opposition to this outrage, those same voices now clamor for a similar intervention in Syria.

"And why shouldn't you arm the Islamists? You know firsthand what good fighters we are," says Abu Hassar. From ear to ear, he grins at me.

He is egging me on, as if he's outfoxed me at a game of checkers and wishes to hustle another round. "No one would accept this idea," I say. "It'd be rejected outright. You're not being serious."

"I don't think we jihadists would have a problem receiving our weapons from the US," he replies.

"It's we Americans who would never accept it! We were fighting each other just two years ago in Iraq."

Now it is Abu Hassar who laughs right in my face. "For your government, it's no worse a position than the one they're in now. We used to be friends, remember—in Afghanistan, in the eighties. If we went from being allies to enemies, that means we can go from being enemies to allies."

"Okay, so how does that end?" I ask. "My government arms the Islamists. Tell me how that ends."

"You really want to know?"

I nod.

"The Prophet predicted all of this," begins Abu Hassar, as if from some place of deep personal knowledge. "He said it starts with the boys, writing and speaking messages of a new future in the streets." Abu Hassar stops and looks at Abed for a moment. By that look, it seems Abed and the Arab Spring's democratic activists were the boys Abu Hassar refers to. "The messages spread, breeding outrage and a war fought by the men. This is what we see now. In that war, an Islamist army rises, uniting to destroy all others. Then a tyrant is killed. This is Assad. His army will fall. Afterward, among the Islamists, there will be many pretenders. The fighting among them will go on."

Abu Hassar glances at my notepad. I haven't been writing anything down. This seems to bother him. "You know all this?" he asks.

"It's all happening right now," I say. "The infighting, the rise of the Islamists. How does that end?"

"The Syrian people thirst for an Islamic state," says Abu Hassar.

"After so much war, they want justice. After Assad falls and when there is fighting among the pretenders, a man will come. He is a common man, but he will have a vision. In that vision, God will tell him how to destroy His enemies and bring peace to all peoples. That man is the Mahdi."

I write down the word *Mahdi*, a heavy and dissatisfied dot above the *i*.

"You don't believe me?" says Abu Hassar.

I stare back at him, saying nothing.

"You think, as poorly armed as we are, we can't defeat Assad and his backers?"

"It's not that," I say.

Abu Hassar continues. "Our weapons don't matter as much as you think. Even Albert Einstein predicted what's happening now. He said that the Third War would be a nuclear war, but that the Fourth War would be fought with sticks and stones. That's how we beat you in Iraq: with sticks and stones. Whether we are helped or not, this is how we will create our Islamic state, even with the superpowers of the world against us."

"So the plan is to wait for the Mahdi?"

"He walks among us now, a simple man of the people, the true redeemer."

I shut my notebook. Our waiter is lurking across the room. I catch his eye and make a motion with my hand, as if I am scribbling out the bill for our lunch. He disappears into the back of the restaurant.

"What will you do if this is true?" Abu Hassar asks me.

"If the Mahdi returns?"

He nods.

"That means there will be a peaceful and just Islamic state?"

Again, he nods.

"Then I'll come visit you with my family."

"And you will be welcome," says Abu Hassar, grinning his wide, ear-to-ear grin and resting his heavy hand on my shoulder.

We've been sitting for hours, and it is early afternoon. Abu Hassar excuses himself to take the day's fourth prayer in a quiet corner of the restaurant. Abed, seemingly exhausted from translating, stands stiffly and goes to use the bathroom. I sit by myself, the empty plates of our lunch spread in front of me.

Our waiter wanders over. "*Syrie?*" he asks, pointing to where Abu Hassar and Abed had been sitting.

I nod.

Then he strokes his face as if he has a thick and imaginary beard, one like Abu Hassar's. "Jabhat al-Nusra," he says.

I shrug.

"*Amerikee?*" he asks, pointing at me, seemingly confused as to why an American would spend so much time sitting with two Syrians, especially one Islamist.

"New York," I say.

He shakes his head knowingly, as if to intone the words *New York* is to intone a universal spirit of *anything goes*.

I hand over the money for lunch. Abed and Abu Hassar return and we leave the restaurant. Outside, the gray morning rain is now gray afternoon rain. The cafés are still full of people sitting on green Astroturf lawns, sipping tea that steams at their lips. Nothing has changed.

We pile into the black Peugeot and return to the road. For a while, we don't speak. We are tired of our own voices. There is just the noise of the broken wiper in front of me, stuttering across the windshield. Above us, the overcast sky loses its light. Below, Akçakale camp spreads in all directions, as gray as a second sky. Something heavy and sad comes over Abu Hassar, and the heaviness of that thing comes over me. He and I have spent the day somewhere else, in a different time. Now he'll go back to the camp and I'll go back to the road.

But we aren't there yet. With about a mile left to go, Abu Hassar puts his hand on my shoulder. "So you will come visit when the war is over?"

"Of course," I say. "If it's safe for someone like me."

"It would have to be. You would never pass for a Muslim." He points at me and speaks to Abed: "He is such a Christian, he even looks like Jesus!"

I glance at myself in the rearview mirror. I haven't shaved in a couple of weeks. My face is a bit gaunt, my kinked hair a bit unkempt. "Maybe I look like Einstein?"

As we pull over by his brother's shop, Abu Hassar and I are still laughing.

"If I look like Jesus," I say, "you look like the Prophet Muhammad."

Abu Hassar shakes his head. "No, I don't look like the Prophet, peace be upon him." He opens his door and a cold breeze fills our car. I can feel the rain outside hitting my neck. Abu Hassar grabs my shoulder with his thick and powerful hands. He pushes his face close to mine. Again he is grinning.

"I look like the Mahdi."

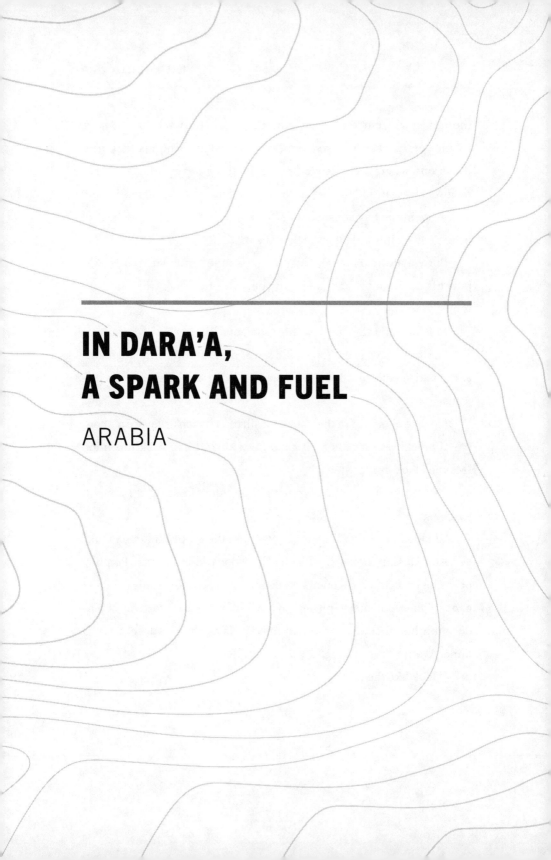

IN DARA'A,
A SPARK AND FUEL

ARABIA

For a revolution to start, it needs a spark, and to spread, it needs fuel. In Syria both have origins in Dara'a, a remote, 3,500-year-old city in the south with fewer than a hundred thousand inhabitants. Dara'a sprouts out of the desert along the Yarmouk River, a tributary branching from the River Jordan that runs to its west. It is an unremarkable place, dusty and poor. Ramshackle tenements stack one upon the other, crowding the streets, their roofs littered with jerry-rigged antennae. Feral dogs roam alleyways that are dank with waste. When the revolution sparks here, Dara'a is saturated with internal refugees from Syria's drought-ridden north, and just as Abu Hassar said, it all starts with the boys writing their messages in the street.

The spark: it's February 22, 2011. Darkness has settled over the city. Six teenagers scribble graffiti on a school wall. "No teaching, no school, until the end of Bashar's rule." The Arab Spring began in the winter, just weeks before, when the twenty-six-year-old Tunisian fruit vendor Mohamed Bouazizi immolated himself in protest after his cart and scales were confiscated by a corrupt government official, and so tonight the boys' actions in Dara'a are laden with Bouazizi's. Another of their messages is less lyrical; it simply reads, "Leave, Bashar." Before they can finish, the boys are arrested. But who catches these nascent revolutionaries? The mukhabarat? Or perhaps the shabiha, those steroid-pumping paramilitaries whose name means "ghosts" and whose loyalty to the government is only surpassed by their loyalty to the Assad family itself?

It's neither of these.

A school guard catches the boys. And this leads to the roundup of fifteen others. They are just teens, but weeks later they haven't been released. Their families petition the local government but to no result. "Forget them," one official says. "If you really want your children, you should make more children. If you don't know how to make more children, we'll show you how to do it." Facing such insults, what's left to do? On March 20, a contagion of anger spreads into the streets of Dara'a, arriving on the doorstep of the al-Omari mosque, built by the grandsons of the Prophet himself, its ancient minaret not cylindrical but famously square. Two years later, after the revolution has metastasized into a war, the regime will destroy this minaret, but now, in its shadow, the police confront hundreds of protestors.

Demonstrations are not without precedent in autocratic Syria: the Kurds in 2005, the Druze in 2000, and as far back as 1982, when Bashar al-Assad's father, Hafez, massacred up to forty thousand citizens and members of the Muslim Brotherhood in Hama. Will this be different? The police kill four protestors. Still, this is nothing new, and when protestors burn the local police station, killing seven officers, this too does not signal the inevitable revolution. So what is the spark? It begins in Dara'a but catches in Damascus, just a few days later, when the people fill both the streets and their throats with these words: "Dara'a is Syria."

To become a flame, a spark needs fuel, and a century's worth of resentment can also be traced to Dara'a.

———

The fuel: on the morning of November 20, 1917, two men in flowing dish-dashas dismount a pair of camels several miles outside of Dara'a. One is an Arab rebel, a bedouin wanderer of little renown, and the other is a British Army officer, Major T. E. Lawrence—or Lawrence of Arabia, as he will famously become known. He has ridden to Dara'a to conduct a re-connaissance of the city's strategic railway junction. For the past year he has played a key role advising the Arab tribes that have revolted against their Ottoman Turkish rulers. The tribes envision a pan-Arabic state, and their leader, Emir Faisal, has successfully united both Sunni and Shiite Muslims to this end. The enemy of my enemy is my friend—so it is and always will be—and with the First World War entering its third year, the Arabs have secured a promise from the British government: help us de-feat our common Turkish adversary and if we are victorious you will be rewarded with an independent Arab state.

Straddling the railway tracks north of the city, Lawrence and his Arab companion set out on foot. For the past year they have fought an irregular and mobile war. Mounted on camels, the insurgent Arabs have raided garrisons and demolished railways and bridges, ravaging supply trains and turning the Turkish rear area into a frontline. If nearly a year of these attacks has taken a toll on the Turks, the year has also taken a toll on the rebels. Lawrence confides in a letter, "I'm not going to last out this game much longer: nerves going and temper wearing thin.... This killing and killing of Turks is horrible." But in addition to the killing, Lawrence is burdened by something else, a secret he carries: the Sykes-Picot Agreement.

A year and a half before Lawrence wanders the train tracks on his reconnaissance of Dara'a, Briton Sir Mark Sykes and French diplomat François Georges-Picot negotiate that in the event of an Allied victory, Arabia will not be for the Arabs, as Lawrence has promised, but will be partitioned into British and French colonial mandates. These secret boundaries draw the lines of present-day Iraq, Syria, and Jordan, carving modern-day discontent into the Middle East with ruler-straight borders that disastrously sever the irregular borders of tribe, religion, and ethnicity. For Lawrence this agreement makes his assurances to Emir Faisal and the united tribes of the Arab Revolt a lie. Lawrence walks the rail line toward Dara'a alongside his Arab companion, burdened by a year's slaughter and the coming betrayal.

The plan had been to scout the tracks leading to Dara'a, but Lawrence brazenly decides to wander into the center of town so he might get a better look at its rail complex. He will hide in plain sight, for who would expect a British Army officer dressed in Arab garb to stroll through the garrisoned streets of Dara'a? The morning's reconnaissance proceeds without incident, but just outside of Dara'a Lawrence strolls past a Turkish army encampment. Who are these two wanderers? And who is this fair-skinned one with blue eyes claiming Circassian descent to explain his whiteness? Lawrence is detained, but his Arab companion is set free.

What happens next is widely disputed among historians, some believing Lawrence's retelling of events and others questioning the accuracy of his account. What seems certain is that the next twenty-four hours forever alter Lawrence, as if the cynicism and brutality he's been surrounded by—the savagery of irregular war, the betrayal embedded in the Sykes-Picot agreement, the dismissiveness of an often-unsupportive British high command—finally erode the optimism fueling his revolt. According to Lawrence, after his capture a Turkish sergeant delivers him to the district governor in Dara'a, a fearsome pederast named Hajim Muhittin. In *Seven Pillars of Wisdom*, Lawrence's classic recounting of the Arab Revolt, he describes the sexual abuse and torture that follows in five explicit and agonizing pages, with passages detailing how the guards "knelt on my ankles, bearing down on the back of my knees, while two more twisted my wrists till they cracked." A blow to the groin "doubled me half-over, screaming, or rather, trying impotently to scream, only shuddering through my open mouth."

After his rape in Dara'a at the hands of Hajim Muhittin, Lawrence is left for dead, allowing him to escape into the desert, where he rendezvouses with his companions. Years on, in 1924, when corresponding with his confidante Charlotte Shaw, the wife of author George Bernard Shaw, Lawrence writes of Dara'a, "About that night. I shouldn't tell you, because decent men don't talk about such things."

Though the Arab Revolt continues for almost another year, *that night* forever marks Lawrence. Ten months later, just weeks before the end of the war, when a column of four thousand Turks and Germans are retreating from Dara'a past the neighboring town of Tafas, Lawrence orders the Arabs under his command to show "no quarter," and he personally supervises the execution of 250 surrendering soldiers. "Then we turned our Hotchkiss [machine gun] on the prisoners and made an end of them, they saying nothing," Lawrence details in his official report. But the events in Dara'a alone are not what seem to take the decency out of the Arab Revolt. Three days after Lawrence's rape, on November 23, 1917, the newly established Bolshevik government in Russia reveals the full text of the Sykes-Picot agreement in the newspapers *Izvestia* and *Pravda*. The exigencies of war will keep Emir Faisal and the Arab tribes fighting on the side of the Allies, but the resentment of their deception and the disastrous carving up of the Middle East to follow become the earliest fuel for the revolution's spark nearly a hundred years later.

———

For a revolution to succeed, the ideals that disrupt the status quo must then become the status quo. This is the point of failure in many uprisings. And it is the point of failure in the Arab Revolt. In 1919, just months after the end of the First World War, Emir Faisal joins Lawrence in Versailles at the Paris Peace Conference to advocate for a pan-Arab state, but in Versailles and in a handful of conferences hosted by colonial powers—San Remo and Cairo—the ideal of pan-Arabism slips away. Sykes-Picot becomes a reality when the British and French cleave the two largest Arab states, Syria and Iraq, out of the lands Faisal once hoped to unite. Acting in defiance, the Syrian Arabs unilaterally proclaim Faisal their king, but both the British and French immediately repudiate this bid for sovereignty. The French assert their mandate over Faisal's independent Syria. Then Faisal marshals an army against them.

But after a swift battlefield defeat on a plain of dust ten miles outside of Damascus, he flees to London, taking shelter among the British, who refused to aid him against this French aggression.

Faisal's reign over Syria lasts four months.

The onetime revolutionary and unifier of Arabs is now an exile, betrayed and then defeated by his old allies. But within the year, the British face unrest in their new mandate of Iraq. In July 1920, the same month Faisal loses his crown in Syria, a revolt against the British begins in Mosul, spreading south along the Euphrates river valley. With their mandate in Iraq crumbling, the British need a strongman who can corral the dissident tribes. Lawrence advocates that his old friend Faisal is just such a leader. Though Faisal is virtually unknown in the new kingdom of Iraq, this hardly matters. Reliability of the man is what's most important. Faisal has learned a lesson in realpolitik, the consequences of acting against British and French interests.

Pragmatic as he's become, Faisal still maintains a certain credibility among Arabs for his leadership in their revolt. With the help of the British, he campaigns among the Iraqis for their support, and within five months a plebiscite—sponsored by the British—unsurprisingly shows 96 percent of Iraqis support Faisal's ascendance to the throne. Thus, in August 1921, thirteen months after losing an independent kingdom in Syria, Faisal is granted a client kingdom in neighboring Iraq. He forms a dynasty that will rule for nearly forty years, until in 1958 a military coup d'état led by Brigadier Abd al-Karim Qasim ousts Faisal's successors. In the turmoil that follows, a young political operative attempts to assassinate Brigadier Qasim the very next year. That operative's name is Saddam Hussein. Within the decade his Ba'ath

Party will rise, and for the remainder of the century a string of strong-men nominally allied with the West will rule in Arabia. Yet the original Arabian strongman was also its original revolutionary: Emir Faisal.

On June 29, 2014, three weeks after the Islamic State begins an offensive that annexes vast swaths of Iraq, its leader, Abu Bakr al-Baghdadi, climbs the minbar in the Great Mosque of al-Nuri in the heart of newly captured Mosul, the same city where Iraqis first revolted against their British occupiers nearly one hundred years before. From this perch al-Baghdadi gazes over the assembled congregants. He wears a black robe and a black turban, the color worn by the Prophet Muhammad during his conquest of Mecca. An electric fan swirls behind him, and beneath the thick tufts of his beard a cluster of microphones are bundled, our only reminders that this image is not from 1,400 years ago. With a grandeur reminiscent of Napoléon's self-coronation, al-Baghdadi has declared himself Caliph Ibrahim Amir al-Mu'minin, "Leader of the Faithful," and he has also declared the establishment of a caliphate straddling present-day Iraq and Syria, stretching toward the Mediterranean Sea and closely matching the borders of the pan-Arab state advocated by T. E. Lawrence and Emir Faisal during their revolt. His remarks are awash with theological references, but when he speaks of the political, his words are meant for Western ears:

> We have now trespassed the borders that were drawn by the malicious hands in the lands of Islam in order to limit our move-

ment and to confine us inside them. And we are working, Allah permitting, to eliminate them. This blessed advance will not stop until we hit the last nail in the coffin of the Sykes-Picot conspiracy.

———

But none of this has happened yet. I am in the car with Abed, our one windshield wiper creaking across the glass, driving back to Gaziantep after our meeting with Abu Hassar. Rain pelts the highway and the New Year, 2014, is only a month off. For a bit longer, the old borders will remain intact.

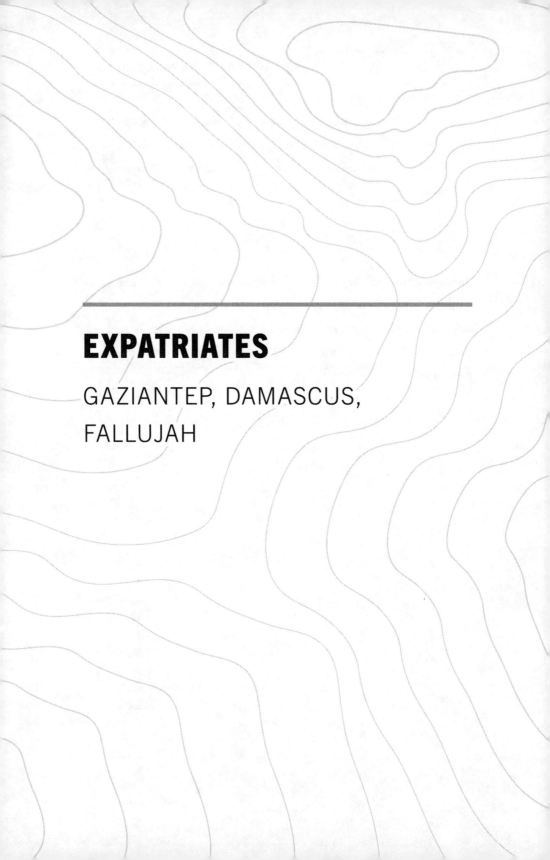

EXPATRIATES

GAZIANTEP, DAMASCUS,
FALLUJAH

The villa's garret is cold, warmed insufficiently by a space heater. Timbers of untreated birch have been nailed into a crosshatch of rafters. Coarse notches in the wood protrude at odd intervals. From them I hang my gym shorts, a towel, a laundry bag. Beneath the rafters I have a bed, piled with a swirl of fleece blankets; also a chair and a desk that face a window, small as a ship's porthole. My view is of Gaziantep's pitched rooftops and a picket of minarets. A week before Christmas they are dusted with snow. Early each morning the muezzins call the first prayer. I am looking forward to sleeping past five a.m., to a few weeks home for the holidays.

Matt is flying home as well, back to Boston. The office will shut down for some days, but Abed will stay. The regime searches for him in Damascus.

More than a year ago, he was called into the army, to fight the rebels. That night the police came to his parents' flat, a walk-up on Mushtahed Street. They carried Abed's draft notice, but Abed wasn't there. Two weeks before, he'd had an argument with his father, a civil servant turned grocery shop owner, who believed Abed's activism was endangering their family. Terrorized by memories of the Hama Massacre in 1982, the tens of thousands of corpses, their arms and legs woven into a bloody carpet along that city's streets, Abed's father told him, "You couldn't walk except by stepping on bodies. You want to take this journey? You will take it by walking over the bodies of your brothers and sisters." Exhausted by such arguments, Abed left home, renting a room in Damascus's old city. And the night when the police shouldered into his parents' doorway, jabbering that the father must sign a receipt for the draft notice of his son, Abed's father refused.

He hung up the phone with his mother, who had told him he must go, and in his dimly lit room Abed packed a bag: two sets of clothes, a USB memory stick, a spiral notebook he'd used as a journal since the revolution's outset, and three books—Fowles's *The French Lieutenant's Woman*, Obama's *Dreams from My Father*, Dickens's *Oliver Twist*. He had twenty-four hours, maybe less, before his conscription notice would flag his detention at the Lebanese border, just a two-hour drive away. But there was one last thing to do. He logged onto Facebook. His sanitized page revealed almost nothing of him: a fake name, archived messages from eighteen months of protests, a profile picture—not his face but a river at sunset. He typed out a quick note to Laetitia, a twenty-four-year-old Swiss woman whom he had met in Damascus the summer before the revolution, during a language exchange where for weeks they had wandered through the old city—the Souq al-Hamidiyya, Nasr Street, the Umayyad mosque—while he spoke Arabic to her so that she might speak French to him.

"I have a problem," he wrote her. "I must leave the country. I want you to know that I love you very much."

He hadn't seen her since it all began, since everything changed, and though they were always in contact, he wondered about those changes. Six months before, he'd asked her to marry him. He didn't have a ring, or enough credit on his phone to even call her in Geneva, so he'd asked in an email. She hadn't answered yet. With a proposal like this, what type of life could they expect? Though he still held out hope.

He logged off and then left his apartment, locking the door behind him.

When Laetitia wrote back, Abed wasn't there to read her response: "I will light a candle for you." And he wasn't there to see her when she broke down and cried.

Abed paid the taxi driver extra to sit in the front seat. Behind him were three others, none of whom he knew. They drove through the darkness, toward the crossing in a wisp of a town called Jdaidit. The taxi's headlights scoured the empty road. They lulled Abed into near hypnosis. Like an athlete before competition, he rehearsed what was to come at the border. His imagination played out a terrifying scene: detention, conscription, torture. Burned onto the memory stick in the small front pocket of his jeans was evidence of his activities, enough to serve as a passport to prison. He took the memory stick from his pocket and slyly tucked it into the passenger-side door. The driver took his eyes from the road. His heavy-lidded gaze rested on Abed and he drove without looking. His stare was fixed, empty, and cold, as if careening into the open desert was an incidental danger when compared to the one Abed had presented him.

"Put that back in your pocket," the driver said.

His voice stabbed and Abed did as he was told, but now he was doubly paranoid: he feared not only the incriminating documents he had sentimentally brought with him but also the suspicion he had incited in the driver. His imagination again played out the scene: the driver waving down a border agent, the two of them speaking and glancing in Abed's direction, the seizure of his passport, his person searched, the incriminating evidence—the memory stick, the journal—and his impotent explanations for both.

The border lights were blinding, the crossing a scrum of sharp elbows and shoves. For a thousand Syrian pounds apiece, about ten US dollars, the driver could assure their passage to Lebanon through a contact. All the passengers assented to pay, though their differing levels of reluctance showed how much this sum meant to them. Then the driver disappeared with their passports, their money. They waited in the taxi.

Abed's imagination continued to race as he opened his door and made his way toward an empty blockhouse of toilets, like those cemented into the rest stops of any major highway. He locked himself in a stall, clutching his journal and memory stick. The driver would return at any moment. There was no time left. Abed made a choice. He ripped the pages from his journal, flushing them down the toilet. In these pages, he had written drafts of the slogans he and the other protestors shouted in the streets: "One, one, one, the Syrian people are one!" And he had written what it felt like to shout those slogans at the police, at the soldiers, at the paramilitaries; to shout in the face of a regime that had muzzled him for his entire life. He flushed the memories away, erasing the descriptions written in his hand. The toilet basins didn't fill quickly enough. He ran between the stalls, flushing all the toilets at once while he ripped the pages. He could hear the noise of those protests swirling in his ears, and now, at this dark crossing, in the quiet, the toilets were too loud. Habitual fear toyed with him. *They will burst in on you, Abed. "What is all this flushing?" they'll say. But I once rushed the barricades at the al-Rifai mosque. I once shouted with my whole voice. But that was then, Abed; now the flushing is too loud.*

Then, quiet; he was finished, and nothing was left—just the flimsy wire of the notebook's spine, which he tossed outside into the dust. He waited at the bathroom door. He still clutched the memory stick, but he would toss that to the ground if he saw a border agent heading toward him. Betrayal was on his mind, the same as a suicide, for what he had just done felt like a bit of both. His body responded: a contortion of sobs that he wrestled down. If the border agent came for him, he must appear indifferent, unfeeling, an innocent. But indifference isn't innocence, he thought. Grief is. After the years of killing, the political setbacks, he had stopped believing in the conscience of an indifferent world, one that had done nothing for Syria. Only those who grieve can be trusted. About this time, though he didn't know it, Laetitia lit her candle for him. Then he saw the driver walking under the border lights, passports in hand, alone. Abed came from the door. He was given his passport. When he saw the stamped page, he finally let go. But the sobs didn't come.

He crossed the border in silence.

Then Beirut, the sea. Strands of neon lights hung from dance clubs. The pockmarked facades of the Barakat building and the Holiday Inn—a once-famous hide for snipers—were reminders of another, older civil war. A telephone. He dialed +41, the Swiss country code, and then her number. "I am safe. I am here."

A steady quiet.

"I am okay," he told her.

"Is it true?"

—

That night just before Christmas, Abed climbs the stairs to my attic room. He's brought a gift, a poem about his home. It reads, in part:

The Damascene House	البيت الدمشقي
Is beyond the architectural text	خارجٌ على نص الفن المعماري
The design of our homes	هندسة البيوت عندنا
Is based on an emotional foundation	تقوم على أساسٍ عاطفي
For every house leans on the hip of another	فكل بيتٍ .. يسند خاصرة البيت الآخر
And every balcony	وكل شرفة
Extends its hand to another facing it	تمد يدها للشرفة المقابله
Damascene houses are loving houses	البيوت الدمشقية بيوتٌ عاشقة
They greet one another in the morning	وتتبادل الزيارات
And exchange visits . . . Secretly—at night	ـ في السر ـ ليلاً

His name, in fact, is not Abed; this is the name he picked for himself during the revolution. The poet is a distant and famous uncle, also an exile, who died far from Damascus, his life spent as an expatriate for other, more provocative words than these. I thank Abed for the gift. Then he returns to his unheated room downstairs.

———

In the first days of the New Year, the Islamic State seizes swaths of al-Anbar Province in Iraq. Their columns shuttle down roads I know well; when I shut my eyes I can still navigate them without a map: Route Bronze to Route Uranium, Route Uranium to Route Michigan—on and on, a net of roads we gave American names to, as if by so naming them we could capture the country in that net.

Masked fighters now stand proudly in the backs of pickup trucks, perched behind machine guns, clutching black flags with the shahadah lashed in curls of white calligraphy: *I bear witness that there is no god but God, and I bear witness that Muhammad is the messenger of God.* They lean on their horns, turning out the crowds—a parade renewed along the streets where I spent my early twenties fighting. In the years since, those streets have never been far from my thoughts. Like Abed and his uncle, I am, and forever will be, living in a strange type of exile, an expatriate of places like Fallujah, Hit, Haditha, and others that barely dot a map. Like any expat, I am defined by a place I might return to someday, the idea that somewhere on my life's horizon is a time when I'll again walk those streets knowing my war is finished.

In reaction to the Islamic State's gains across al-Anbar, a chorus of pundits wonders about the cost of America's war in Iraq. Marines I fought alongside are quoted in newspapers across the country. They appear on television programs, their voices wrestling with a single question: *Was it all a waste?* I have a hard time pinning down my emotions about this. Instead a memory keeps looping in my mind, flickering like old archive footage.

It is my birthday. It is also Corporal Pratt's, Sergeant Banotai's, Lance Corporal Ames's, and Lieutenant Dan Malcom's. We sit in a column of fourteen armored personnel carriers, called amtracks, nearly two hundred of us. It is November 10, 2004, the Marine Corps' 229th birthday. Hydraulic wiring threads our amtrack's steel interior compartment, sweating oil, which drips onto helmets, night-vision goggles, rifles, assault packs. A blue infrared light illumines the confines, casting an icy glow against our faces, as if we're all trapped beneath a frozen lake. We exchange whispers of "happy birthday, Marine," which is the custom. We are four kilometers outside of Fallujah, the city of mosques: a forest of minarets rising from kaleidoscopic facades, all mosaicked in bursting hexagonal patterns of turquoise, crimson, and cobalt. Our single company is part of the First Marine Division, a force of thousands. Within minutes, our column will ride into the heart of the city to seize the Government Center, a walled complex of five buildings defended by the Islamic State's precursor, al-Qaeda in Mesopotamia. Our amtrack lurches into gear, jostling a few of us onto the deck plates. The radio squelches to life, and I recognize the voice of our executive officer reading the traditional birthday message crafted by General John A. Lejeune nearly a hundred years before:

> On November 10, 1775, a Corps of Marines was created by a resolution of the Continental Congress. Since that date many thousand men have borne the name Marine. In memory of them it is fitting that we who are Marines should commemorate the birthday of our Corps by calling to mind the glories of its long and illustrious history.

Through the inches-thick glass of the amtrack's armored cupola, I peer into darkness. The city in front of us is on fire. The radio is silent. And I swear to God I can hear all of us breathing.

Two weeks before the battle, they pulled us into a camp just outside of the city. We were supposed to prepare, but instead we waited. When we arrived there was nowhere for us to stay, no barracks, no tents. The logistics officers showed us to a series of vehicle service bays, long garages where Saddam Hussein's army once maintained its trucks. The soft earth around the bays was planted with unexploded cluster bombs, remnants of last year's invasion, and we made sure only to walk on the paved roads. The noise of brooms sweeping up broken glass and rubble filled the camp as we worked with T-shirts tied around our faces so we wouldn't inhale the great clouds of dust that varnished our sweating limbs with a film of grime. Then we showered by holding liter bottles of water over one another's heads.

The assault would begin on D-Day, and it made us nervous that we would be part of a D-Day. We memorized our orders: what would happen on D plus one, D plus two, and so on. Truth be told, the plan didn't extend in any real detail past that first day, when our company would seize the Government Center, with its symbolic significance in the heart of the city. After that, no one really knew.

A concrete porch with a corrugated steel overhang circled each of the garages where we slept. From these porches a steady hum of conversation rose up each evening. Perched on collapsible camp chairs and field stools, with our rifles and machine guns stacked like teepees and our floppy bush hats and vagrant stares, we assumed the air of modern-day Hatfields and McCoys, well-armed idlers awaiting the violence coded into our DNA. During those days of waiting, Ames, my radio operator, a kid who smelled like old socks, looked like he should've been in the National Guard, and sounded like he had a stuffy nose, would charge batteries and clean dust off his radio's connections with a pencil eraser. He liked to talk politics and speculated that if in a few days John Kerry won the presidential election, the assault might get called off. Although several of us explained to him that the inauguration wouldn't be until January, he still thought there was a chance. Banotai and Pratt, two noncommissioned officers, would pitilessly make the younger Marines inventory and reinventory their assault packs, counting out rockets, grenades, and types of ammunition with names like HE, HE/DP, 5.56 link, 5.56 ball, Willie Pete, AT-4. Across a dirt courtyard, in a garage just like ours, was the company headquarters. Dan, the weapons officer who controlled air strikes and artillery for our company, would sit out here, a portable magnetic chessboard balanced on an upturned case of MREs. Dan spoke with a smooth Virginia drawl—when he spoke, which wasn't that often. On the weekends back in Camp Lejeune, he didn't trawl bars like Rumrunners and Squeakies, or strip clubs like Cherry's or the Driftwood. Instead he spent his evenings at Books-A-Million and began dating the register girl, a sturdily built blonde who, if I remember correctly, stood a bit taller than him.

When the assault's estimated casualty figures slipped out, I was sitting with Dan one evening, losing at chess. Seventy percent—that's what the planners expected. I don't know how the number leaked to all of the Marines; probably some lance corporal saw it on a PowerPoint slide and told one of his buddies, who told another in turn. Rumors in the infantry spread from the bottom up, and official information from the top down. The most sensitive plans and orders are often mulled over for days at the higher levels of command, among the generals and colonels, before they're passed down to the captains and lieutenants. But there's always some kid on the staff, a private or a lance corporal, who will overhear a conversation, see a briefing, and let out the word.

As a young officer, I quickly learned that if all of the junior Marines were walking around with a hangdog expression, they'd heard of something going on at higher headquarters that I wasn't privy to yet. Usually I'd find Ames, who was tapped into the underground mill of lance corporal rumors, and more often than not, my orders would filter up through him a couple of days before they'd filter down. This made us a bit of a team: him looking down, me looking up, neither of us really understanding what was coming our way.

Dan didn't think much of the 70 percent figure. He kept staring at the board between us, stroking his chin with long, tapered fingers that seemed designed to pluck at chess pieces. I asked if we could finish the game later—I thought I should gather up the Marines in my platoon and talk to them about the estimated casualty rate, a little *don't worry, you're not going to die* pep talk.

"What good's that going to do?" Dan asked.

"Maybe make them feel better," I said.

"The only way to make them feel better," he answered, "is to make them not think at all."

For a fighting man, the imagination is a dangerous trap: painful ways to die, life-shattering wounds, your grieving family—these are all too easy to conjure, so either shut off your imagination or succumb to it. For the rest of our chess game, that's what I struggled to do, unsuccessfully wrestling the figure from my thoughts. *Seventy percent, seventy percent.* There were forty-six of us in the platoon: thirty-two of us would end up casualties; fourteen wouldn't. Those sums replaced seventy. The odds were probably a bit worse for me, if I was being honest. The lieutenants always get picked off. The guy running down the street waving his arms, shouting orders into a radio, trying to get everyone to move in the same direction—that's the guy you want to shoot. Ames's odds were probably a bit worse than mine. That radio would be strapped to his back, a ten-foot antenna wobbling upward from his spine.

When Dan called checkmate, my mind was barely in the game and I couldn't recount the series of moves that'd led me into this position. No options existed for me. A pile of my pieces lay stacked by Dan's side of the board. I quickly counted them, trying to add up what percentage of my army he'd had to destroy before it was all over.

———

Our amtracks sprint toward the Government Center, and the other companies are calling medevacs across the radio, moving out their casualties. "This is Cajun 3. I have two priorities at the intersection of Phase Line Henry and Juliet, over!" Or, "This is Beowulf 1. Three urgents, one routine, at the intersection of Phase Line George and Eleanor, over!" In the background of these transmissions, the loud static *crack* of gunfire interrupts the idling radio's low static hum. Like two mirrors placed opposite another, each medevac reflects the one before it, creating an impression that bends outward toward infinity. Medevacs have three classifications: routine, priority, urgent. Routine medevacs are for two things: a very minor wound, which in the heat of battle likely won't warrant a medevac, and the dead. Death has a low priority. Why conduct a risky medevac for a body? Protocol demands that only number, location, and type of medevac are passed over the radio—no names. You can't function if you turn the priorities, routines, and urgents into so many people.

Now the city is dark. The fires that burned in front of us are gone. We've moved beyond the corridor that the other two companies had fought all day to open for our advance. It is quiet and I strain to make out the barrier between the sky and the looming, motionless buildings. I place my night-vision goggles up to the cupola's glass. Many of the homes have had whole walls lopped off clean, so they open to my view like dollhouses, their sofas, chairs, and beds upturned and rearranged as if a petulant child, becoming bored with nice play, had shaken them. Our column stops and the amtracks' engines idle warmly in the dark. I remove my night-vision goggles and hear, but don't see, the whine of two tanks as they rush past. Then a blossom of sparks, followed by a low, rhythmic pounding. More sparks. More pounding. With their main guns, the tanks are punching holes in the cement wall that surrounds the Government Center.

I climb down from my seat beneath the cupola, into the troop compartment. Everyone is standing, facing the back ramp, burdened under the loads Pratt and Banotai had checked and rechecked. Our amtrack jars forward, lumbering toward the breach the tanks are shooting into the Government Center's outer wall. Like rush-hour commuters in a crammed subway car, we strain to grab something that might steady us—a piece of the armored hull, a handle, each other. From night-vision goggles, two coins of green demon light project onto a dozen sets of eyes that are all very open.

Then everything is still.

A hydraulic wheeze. The back ramp drops.

Our platoon had planned to clear four of the five buildings inside the Government Center: a school, a six-story building called the "high-rise," and, on the farthest, southern side of the compound, a pair of identical buildings we'd christened Mary-Kate and Ashley, an homage to the Olsen twins. After issuing these orders, my company commander, a lanky career officer named Cunningham, whose voice I wouldn't recognize if it wasn't partly muffled by the enormous chaw of tobacco he habitually chewed, pulled me aside. "I don't expect you guys to make it through all four buildings." I stared at him for a moment, a little confused. Cunningham was a fair commander who didn't dole out undeserved criticism. Even though we had our problem children, Marines who never seemed to get anything right, I felt a bit hurt that he didn't think our platoon could complete this task. Then he added, "I don't think you guys will be combat-effective by the end." And I understood—it was that number, 70 percent. Cunningham then outlined a plan only I should know of, in which another platoon would backfill us once we'd sustained too many casualties to go further. He then took me over to the battalion headquarters, where the intelligence section had a few minutes of video filmed clandestinely by a cabbie who had driven our route into the city. The film was out of focus and shaky, as if the cabbie were either drunk or terrified when he took it.

After watching the video, I stepped outside. Our entire battalion, several hundred of us, gathered in a circle around a three-star general and a sergeant major, the two senior-most Marines in Iraq at the time. They'd come to deliver their own pep talk before the assault. They said some stuff about Fallujah being an iconic battle, like Belleau Wood, Iwo Jima, or the Chosin Reservoir, names our Marine Corps selves had grown up on as surely as our civilian selves had grown up on *Full House*. Then the sergeant major, a fit guy in his late forties whose trim physique and perfectly shaved head demonstrated an equal contempt for fat and hair, paced around the assembled group, arms crossed, as television cameras from our embedded journalists rolled. "Now this is what I'm talkin' 'bout. This is a whole can of whoop-butt! It is an honor for me to be able to serve with each and every one of you hard chargers. . . . You going to go in there and do what you always have done: kick butt!"

After the speech, everyone walked back to the garages. Dan found me in the crowd. "The skipper discuss the backup plan with you?" he asked. I nodded, not really wanting to talk about it anymore. "What'd you think about the speech?" I asked him. Dan shrugged. "If a bunch of us are going to get killed, you'd think the sergeant major might say *ass* in front of the cameras."

Our assault meets with silence. The Government Center has been abandoned. In the darkness our platoon clears its four buildings against no resistance. But the city awakes to gunfire. Between machine gun salvos, rockets, and grenades, the Marines snap pictures of each other with cheap disposable cameras. No one's been hurt yet.

Our platoon is spread between Mary-Kate and Ashley. The two rooftops are flat and rimmed with a chest-high wall. The steady *whip-crack* of rifle fire passes above our heads all morning. The sky is perfectly blue, and in front of us is Highway 10. Its four lanes bisect the city. Back in March, dozens of cheering Fallujans dragged the charred and dismembered remains of four Blackwater contractors down this highway. For three days their bodies hung from the crossbeams of the Euphrates Bridge.

By around nine a.m., all hell is breaking loose. Rocket-propelled grenades sail overhead regularly, like trains passing through a station. One slams into a wall behind us. Everyone is okay. A piece of steel, jagged as a shark's tooth, embeds into Pratt's groin protector. Smoke rises from the Kevlar flap. Pratt waves it away. He's fine. Ames takes a picture. We all laugh, sort of.

Across the Government Center, on the roof of the high-rise, Cunningham and Dan set up their radios. They call in air strikes. Overhead, that perfect blue sky now swarms with attack helicopters and jets. Like herons taking fish from the sea, they swoop down and gulp whole buildings from the city. When their bombs drop close, we press ourselves against the roof's wall and open our mouths so the overpressure won't rupture our eardrums. Soon Cunningham announces they're moving off the high-rise's roof, and in the background of his transmission I can hear the *buzz-snap* of the rifle fire that's forcing him down to the lower floors.

Despite the November chill, I've sweat through my uniform completely. Even my boots are wet. I look at my watch: 0917. I decide to stop looking at my watch. I'll never make it through the day if I do.

Our building shakes on its foundation. Steel hits its side like the crack of a thousand bullwhips. I lose sight of the Marines around me. We disappear into a cloud of dust. When the dust clears, half the platoon have their mouths open. It's too late, though, and my ears ring and hurt. Ames screams, "What the fuck was that, LT?"

"Fucking Muj artillery!" says Pratt.

"The Muj don't have fucking artillery," I say. "That's ours."

I grab the radio's handset and call Dan, who along with Cunningham is now off the high-rise's roof and a couple of stories down. "I didn't call that artillery in," Dan says in his soft Virginia drawl.

Before I can say *Shit, who did?* another salvo lands right in front of us. It tears open Highway 10, tossing surfboard-sized hunks of asphalt skyward. The air sucks out so hard, it feels like an open palm smacked across my cheek. Among the forty-six of us, I hear someone whimper. I crawl over to Ames. Broken glass and cement crunch beneath my palms and knees. I grab the radio again. We're pressed together so closely, I can see every pimple on his nineteen-year-old face. Before I can scream at Dan, he tells me the artillery is coming from our regimental headquarters far outside of the city. And he says, calmly, "I'm headed to the roof to get it shifted off you."

I throw the handset back at Ames. I feel forty-six sets of eyes on me. There is a strange quiet. We're pressed shoulder to shoulder. Some pigeons land on our rooftop, look at us, then quickly fly off. It's as if we and the insurgents all anxiously await the next artillery salvo.

Far away, I hear a single gunshot, an insignificant *pop.*

Immediately, all hell breaks loose again, as if sound has suddenly refused to travel through time and decided to tear off wherever it pleases. We press into the wall, but our ears don't hurt, no dust consumes us. I poke my head up. About a hundred yards away, the artillery impacts land among the insurgents' positions.

I grab the radio. "Nice shooting!" I tell Dan.

Cunningham's voice meets mine. "Get a corpsman to the high-rise."

Dan was the first one killed that day.

I didn't check my watch again until that night. It read *2350,* and we'd crossed Highway 10, fighting almost 400 meters deeper into the city. Of the forty-six on the rooftop that morning, twenty-five were still on their feet. We didn't know it then, but we'd fight in Fallujah for another month. And we would exceed 70 percent.

———

I wear a black steel bracelet on my wrist. It's got Dan's name on it, and the date November 10, 2004. I wear it for him, but for others too. Next to that bracelet is another, a plastic one threaded with pink hearts and blue stars that my three-year-old daughter made for me. If it weren't for the steel bracelet, the plastic one wouldn't exist.

When I think about my wars, and what happened, I do sometimes ask myself if it was worth it. But I'm not thinking about Bush or Obama, or about Iraq or Afghanistan. I'm thinking about Pratt and Ames, and of course Dan, and unfortunately other friends like him. I wonder what they'd say. I hope they'd think what we did for each other was worth it.

———

After the holidays, Matt and his staff return to work—ginning up business, bidding on contracts, taking research trips to the border and the constellation of refugee camps that straddle it. In the evenings we eat cross-legged on a carpet in the living room, inside a concentric circle of space heaters. We all take turns cooking. Heather, a Turkish and Arabic speaker from the Pacific Northwest, proves adventurous in her tastes, picking dead bees from the whole honeycomb she buys at the market, or ordering fresh yogurt to our residence, delivered in a steel pail by a farmer she's befriended. She endures bouts of food poisoning in good spirits. Kristine, a blonde from Minnesota who speaks Arabic so well it turns heads, subsists on a diet of salted popcorn. After dinner we all play Scrabble. Some nights we drink at local bars, neon-lit basement joints. One night at the Tuğcan Hotel, cloaked in a disco ball's orbit of light, I sing karaoke: "Losing My Religion."

Across the border, the situation deteriorates further. The Islamic State seizes its new capital in Syria's Ar-Raqqah governorate. The rapidity of these setbacks awes much of the international community. The Islamic State's success can be attributed to many factors: the corruption and inefficacy of the Free Syrian Army, the Maliki government's refusal to integrate Sunnis into the fabric of political life, and the lack of a residual US force in Iraq. Though fundamentally these factors can be reduced to one: a power vacuum.

That extremists would step into a power vacuum is no surprise. It happened with the Taliban in the 1990s and with al-Qaeda in Mesopotamia in the past decade. In this part of the world, extremism is not a *fait accompli*. It has been brought about by a certain set of conditions: lawlessness, sectarian violence, corruption. These create fertile ground for radical ideologies to take root. All these negative strains exist within Iraq and Syria. Abu Bakr al-Baghdadi, the self-proclaimed caliph of the Islamic State, fought against the United States in the Iraq War, rising to become the chief of al-Qaeda in Mesopotamia in May 2010. In 2011, when Abed and other activists took to the streets across Syria, Abu Bakr's organization appeared to be in its final throes. Then, in a collapsing Syria, it was offered the exact opportunity it needed. Just as the US invasion of Iraq and the toppling of Saddam Hussein's regime created a power vacuum to be filled by international jihadis, so, too, has the democratically minded Syrian revolution. For Abed and me, our wars each devolved into disasters for the same reason: by trying to unleash sweeping change in the region, we created the conditions for extremists to rise.

At times, sitting out on the veranda after a meal, I hear him say that he regrets his revolution and he wishes that he—and, by implication, his generation—had never taken to the streets in protest. At other times, I hear him say he has no regrets: that the struggle isn't over, and any chance to live in a free society is worth the suffering. He wrestles with the good and the bad, the duality within the defining political and emotional event of his life. After watching the Islamic State's reemergence in Iraq, I now recognize the same duality in my experience.

Like his uncle, Abed is a poet. After one such conversation, he shares "Take Me," some verse he composed on December 9, 2011, the Friday of the Dignity Strike, one of a series of planned nonviolent protests during the heady, early days of the revolution:

> *I've taken my decision, put my olives and bread in the baskets,*
> *and stay awake praying for me, Mother, as long as the moon is up.*
> *I am lost for words to express*
> *my overwhelming happiness to have an appointment with history*
> *while carrying with me water for the rebels.*

A few days later, I ask Abed more about this poem, what it meant to him, whether he still feels the same. "Back then, I was coordinating the protests in Damascus and the rebels were seizing ground in the countryside," he says. "All of us were bound by this platonic love of freedom. We felt like we were making history."

"Do you think there's some young member of the Islamic State marching to Baghdad now, glamorizing his appointment with history?" I ask.

"Sadly," he says, "it's something we all have in common."

A PRAYER FOR AUSTIN TICE

DAMASCUS, ISTANBUL,
WASHINGTON, D.C.

She counts the Tuesdays. By the spring of 2014, her total creeps toward one hundred. To mark the weeks since she last heard from her son, she posts photos of him online. The final message before his Twitter feed went silent came on a Sunday: "Spent the day at an FSA pool party with music by @taylorswift13. They even brought me whiskey. Hands down, best birthday ever."

Achievement always marked his path: Eagle Scout, then the Marine Corps—Iraq and Afghanistan—then Georgetown Law. Then Syria. He'd decided to go there as a freelance journalist between his second and third years of law school. While classmates jockeyed for internships at firms, Austin Tice booked a flight to Istanbul. In May 2012, summer started and Austin packed a bag and a camera, then left.

When he disappeared that August, a flurry of questions followed in the media and among Marines who'd known him or known of him. At first they were the obvious ones: *Who's holding him? Who saw him last?* But then other, larger questions emerged, and eventually they distilled into one: *Why'd he go?*

———

Along the periphery of Syria's civil war, I often meet veterans of the last decade's wars, wanderers amidst the Arab Spring's upheaval. Places like Tahrir, Aleppo, Tunis, and Taksim possess a new and yet familiar allure, promising to replace names we've let go: Ramadi, Helmand, Haditha, Khost. When we meet, we talk about the other things we're doing: field researcher, writer, photojournalist, whatever. Our current "professions" are often described with a shrug of the shoulders, followed by a spell of silence, as if our true profession is the unspoken one—the one we left behind.

When I first meet Vince, a Marine turned English teacher, in a bar off Istanbul's Taksim Square, I ask him what type of certificate he needs to teach and what materials he uses with his students. He laughs at me. "You don't need a certificate." Then he leans in close, over the bottle of wine I'm splitting with him and his Cypriot girlfriend. "The guys are obsessed with Victoria's Secret." He explains how it's the most compelling material he can find for his all-male students at their conservative religious school. "It's all they want to talk about," he tells me. "It is a conversation class."

While transiting Istanbul, I had received a message from Vince over Twitter, asking if I wanted to meet. His profile picture is of a gaunt twentysomething, unshaven, a shadow of stubble cast against his pale skin. He wears an old T-shirt with a stretched collar, and he sits on a Persian carpet, leaning against a bookshelf as he stares upward, toward what must be the ceiling light. But the photograph's style implies that he is staring somewhere more profound. Perhaps I agree to meet him to see if this is true.

As an infantryman, Vince fought in Ramadi between 2005 and 2007, some bloody years. Perched on my stool in the bar, I ask when he started coming to the Middle East. "The first thing I did when I got out of the Marines," he says, "was to buy a ticket back here." While we work through another bottle, Vince's girlfriend grows bored of our conversation. She leans her head against the wall, shuts her eyes, and naps while Vince speaks passionately about his Syrian friends, many of whom he's lost track of since the war started.

He asks if I've ever been to Lebanon. I haven't, but my old infantry battalion garrisoned the airport in Beirut when Hezbollah detonated a truck bomb at their barracks in 1983, killing 241 Marines, sailors, and soldiers. It was the Corps' bloodiest single day since Iwo Jima. Vince nods when I tell him. "You were with one-eight," he says, and it feels good to be speaking our common language.

He starts another story, about a trip he took to a coastal town in southern Lebanon. "That's Hezbollah country. And here I am, this jarhead walking around bare-chested and pasty white." He pats his left shoulder. "I have a big eagle, globe, and anchor here." He lifts his shirt. Inked onto his ribs is a single rifle bayoneted into the dirt, with names listed on a scroll: his dead friends. "I can't remember the last time I felt as proud as I did walking down that beach."

Our waiter comes over. Vince nudges his girlfriend, asking her if she wants something to eat. She shakes her head, then leans it back against the wall and shuts her eyes again. The two of us order hamburgers.

Then Vince tells me another story, about how in January 2011 he was back in the States, going to college in Chicago. On a Wednesday, as he came out of class, his Twitter feed exploded with news from friends in Cairo. An enormous protest was planned in Tahrir Square after midday prayers as part of what would later be known as the Friday of Rage.

"This was the revolution," he explains. "It was going to be the largest protest in Egypt's history." That night he bought a flight from O'Hare, and he landed in Cairo on Thursday. By Friday, he was in the square. "I had this idea that I'd live-tweet the entire thing," says Vince. "Then they shut Twitter down, so I was just in it." In the course of a day, Egyptian security services nearly arrested him for taking photos, and the Muslim Brotherhood nearly kidnapped him for being an American. "The whole time those guys held me, I kept telling them, 'Egyptian people are good, Egyptian government is bad. American people are good, American government is bad.'" By Saturday, Vince had returned to the airport. He managed to get on an evacuation flight organized by the US State Department. By Tuesday, he was back in class.

"It made me the coolest guy in my creative writing seminar," he says, finishing his food. "But I had no business being there."

We settle the bill, and the three of us step outside for a smoke. The cool air brings a snap of sobriety, and I ask him, "Why are you here?"

He looks back at me as if I should know. As if he should ask me the same.

We stroll through Taksim Square. In June 2013, the previous summer, Prime Minister Recep Tayyip Erdoğan ordered police to forcefully disperse a few dozen environmental activists who squatted in nearby Gezi Park protesting development plans for the public land. Long criticized for his autocratic style and Islamist tendencies, Erdoğan provoked tens of thousands of Turks to flood into Taksim, turning the barren square into a lake of protestors, chanting, singing, grinding Istanbul to a standstill that only eased beneath clouds of CS gas, which left behind a bitterness that lingered in the tight lanes and grottoes of the old city for days, wafting up now and again at the passing of a strange breeze.

As we wander by Galatasaray Lisesi, a high school dating back to the fifteenth century and a congregation point for demonstrations, the police remain out in force. Their plastic riot shields lean against their legs, and they wear fiberglass breastplates similar to those worn by motocross riders, their batons slung at their sides. I ask Vince why he's settled in Istanbul. He talks a bit about his job, the parts of the city he likes, the parts of other cities he doesn't like. But in the end he settles on "To be close to *it*."

It's the same *it* many of us need to be close to.

This isn't a cause, although it can be. This isn't a particular war, but it's often that too. If I were to describe *it*, I'd say it's an experience so large that you shrink to insignificance in its presence. And that's how you get lost in *it*.

When Austin Tice was kidnapped, he was about as close as you can get to *it*.

———

That so many of us went to war in this part of the world, only to return, seems no surprise. For some of us, the wars have gone on so long that we lack context for a life outside of them. While home in the States that past January, I had met up with an old friend, a veteran special operator whom I've known since my early twenties. He's still deploying and has been since the invasion of Iraq in 2003, so I'll just call him Jack. With both of us back for the holidays, Jack and I reunited for a jog, as we customarily do. As we ran through Washington, D.C., past the monuments, through the gentrifying neighborhoods, we talked about PTSD and whether we have it or not. He asked if I ever had dreams. I told him no, but that I sometimes get very sad. An idea, a memory, will suddenly come to mind, stopping me cold. When this happens, life feels like a brutal Hallmark commercial played on a loop. I usually wind up crying.

Jack has dreams. And one keeps repeating.

He's on a raid. It's dark—the middle of the night. His team of Marines blows an explosive charge through the front door of a compound. He's with the first group, clearing the structure. Suddenly he's alone. He enters a room, and there's a guy with an AK-47 in it. The guy levels his rifle. Jack shoots back, but there's only a hollow *click*. He's out of ammunition. He reaches into his vest to do a speed reload. He goes for a magazine, but he pulls out a ham sandwich instead. He reaches into another magazine pouch. Another ham sandwich.

"All I've got are ham sandwiches," he said, and we both laughed.

Then he looked over at me. "I wake up and I'm fucking scared."

Neither of us talked for a bit.

Dreams, an intense weight of sadness—these manifestations of our wartime experience could surely be classified as PTSD, but the more insidious form of PTSD is the purposelessness associated with giving up the war. To be happy one must have a sense of purpose. Let's take a conventional example: a man works a job, that job supports his family, it allows him to save a bit of money, his family grows, with his savings they go to university, his children have a better life than him. He is valued. He has a purpose. From that purpose he finds happiness. But a young soldier who goes to war has a formative experience that gives him a very different and intense relationship with purpose. Let's say he's fighting in a remote valley, at a desert outpost, in an urban hellhole—the details don't really matter. He's got a mission, the same as the other soldiers who have become his close friends. This soldier fights for that mission but also to protect these friends. This is a very potent type of purpose. If purpose is the drug that induces happiness, there are few stronger doses than the wartime experience. The soldier leaves home at a young age and begins taking this strongest drug, in effect freebasing the crystal meth of purpose. But eventually the war ends, the soldier returns home. He must reintegrate into society, find his happiness. Find a new purpose. He evaluates his options: a job at Home Depot, going to college, working in real estate. Nothing compares to what he's just done. He looks around and his world is no longer crystal meth. His world is Coors Light. A certain depression sets in: the knowledge that the rest of his days will be spent sitting on his front porch, sipping Coors Light, watching life pass by. This emotional arc isn't unique to the veteran: professional athletes, artists with great early success—anyone who's viewed the peak must reckon with the descent.

Jack and I continued our run.

Stopped at a traffic light, we jogged in place. I told him I missed the war.

He nodded.

"You know, Ack, the melancholy of it all is that we grew up there."

———

I never knew Austin Tice. I'm sure he went to Syria for many reasons. But I imagine he missed the war in the way I do. The way Vince does. I imagine it's never far from his mind, the way it is with Jack on our runs.

The road home from battle has always been fraught. When Odysseus journeyed back from Troy, his men tied him to the mast of his ship when the Sirens tempted him to leave it. The goddess Circe warned Odysseus about these sea nymphs:

> . . . whoever comes their way. Whoever draws too close,
> off guard, and catches the Sirens' voices in the air—
> no sailing home for him, no wife rising to meet him,
> no happy children beaming up at their father's face.
> The high, thrilling song of the Sirens will transfix him.

Odysseus ordered his men to stuff their ears with beeswax as they rowed by. He didn't, though. He wanted to hear the Sirens. Lashed down, he listened. It wasn't their honeyed voices or unrivaled beauty that made him strain against the mast. It was what they sang of: war, and man's glory in war.

Aside from a brief YouTube video released in September 2012, virtually nothing's been seen or heard of Austin Tice. Many speculate that the Assad regime is holding him, but who knows. As I drift around southern Turkey and the Syrian border, I sometimes pull up his dormant Twitter feed on my phone, thumbing through Tweets like "@kenentrepreneur No, unless you count Facebook ranting about my time in Iraq/Afghanistan. I'm a total rookie; a law student on summer vacay," or "FSA company commander: 'Is that a joke? Of course we don't care about the Olympics.'"

It sounds like he was living out a dream: bearing witness to a cause he believed in. A part of me admires him for it, despite where it led.

Then I'll scroll to his profile. Beneath "#USMC infantry vet, #Georgetown Law stdnt, freelance #journalist. Currently in #Syria" are these words, written like a prayer:

Gaze into the abyss,
the abyss gazes also into you.

BLACK IN THE RAINBOW, BERGDAHL AND THE WHALE

ISTANBUL, PAKTIKA, QUANTICO

S ummer, and the LGBT Pride Festival comes to Istanbul, beginning with the fifth annual Trans Pride march along Istiklal Caddesi. How will the spiritual capital of this majority-Muslim country sustain an unabashed expression of nonconventional sexuality, especially one set on its most iconic thoroughfare? The idea of the Istiklal, one of the renowned neoclassical *grande rues*, bedecked with rainbow flags is allure enough. With the Islamic State advancing to the south toward Baghdad beneath the black banners of martyrdom, this march seems a fine barometer of the political pressures inside the gateway to the Islamic world. Or at least, a counterpoint.

With an afternoon sitter scheduled for my kids, I hitch the bus from my flat in Bebek, a gentrified neighborhood up the Bosporus, down the seaside highway toward Cihangir District, the heart of the city and the location of the June 2013 Gezi Park demonstrations, a brief, if intense, uncorking of Turkish political dissent partly inspired by the Arab Spring. I've planned to meet Vince and Nate, a tall former army officer with bushy red hair who is fresh out of the service and on an extended world tour. Arriving in Taksim Square, I run right into rows of plainclothes policemen. They chatter into their walkie-talkies, ready to deploy. Across the square, the footsteps of casual shoppers echo off the Istiklal's cobblestones.

The march will begin at five. At around half past four, I link up with Vince, who has brought his girlfriend, and Nate. Before we can finish our greetings, the sound of whistles and drums picks up from the Istiklal. We head toward its mouth. Instead of being swept up by the protest's current, we hit a countercurrent composed of hundreds of shoppers pouring out into Taksim Square. Beyond them, I can see an enormous rainbow flag, maybe seventy by ten meters, unfurled in the street. The shoppers hurry from it like they're in B-roll footage from an old Godzilla film, trying to avoid the march. We draw closer and fall in with the protestors. Activists press pastel green, pink, and red paddles into our hands with slogans like *#Transcandir* (#Transgender) and *Anayasada Cinsiyet Kimliği* (Gender Identity Is in the Constitution). Mustachioed Turks in threadbare suit pants and short-sleeve shirts hawk an assortment of whistles for two lira per, taking breaks from their usual commerce of knockoff designer bags and watches. A few minutes before the hour, the marchers lift their flag, taking turns dancing beneath its luminescent shade. A phalanx of Turkish police, plastic riot shields at the ready, batons slung at their sides, fan out behind us.

When Nate, Vince, and I decided to head down to the Istiklal, my initial concern was that we'd stick out: two former Marines and a soldier at a Turkish transgender pride march. Not so much, as it turns out. Most of the crowd isn't transgender. This is a march for that community's rights, but it is really just a march for rights. Clutching a few inches of the silk flag, I glance across to its other side, where a dour Turk in his sixties wears an elegant, trim sports coat and a white straw fedora. He walks steadily, slowly surveying the crowd from behind a pair of dark glasses. He seems to march alone, speaking to no one. I wonder what tethers him to this cause.

At that point Nate, whom I've only just met, leans over and asks me to snap a picture of him and Vince. "My sister's transgender," he says.

Since Gezi Park, other protests have regularly shut down parts of the city. A few weeks ago I found myself in the center of three widely different demonstrations in a three-day period. The first was a gathering of several hundred supporters of deposed Egyptian president Mohamed Morsi outside the Egyptian consulate in Bebek, where I live. I had heard chanting from my living room window a little before ten p.m. When I went to check things out, I found myself in a sea of Islamists waving yellow flags emblazoned with the black four-finger salute of the Rabaa Massacre, the square where 2,600 Muslim Brotherhood supporters had been beaten and gunned down by security forces the summer before. Feeling a bit uncomfortable, I did the least threatening thing I could: I bought an ice-cream cone from my local concessionaire. The crowd soon spread onto the playground where I take my children after kindergarten. I finished my cone while the protestors standing on the plastic blue slide of the jungle gym chanted, *"Allahu Akbar!"* The next afternoon, I came home to another cry for activism: Toms Shoes. They were hosting a "Go Shoeless for a Day" rally in the same park. While my kids ate cotton candy and popcorn, a barefooted Turkish soap opera star vaulted onto a hastily erected stage, interrupting the DJ to make a few remarks about how by going without shoes we could all better understand the struggles of the impoverished. The crowd cheered from the playground with just as much enthusiasm as *Allahu Akbar*. The next morning was May Day. Determined to keep an appointment, I ventured out into the streets. The police had closed nearly every main avenue into the city center. I managed to find what I thought was a clever back route, but got turned around and eventually ended up getting tear-gassed alongside members of the TKP, or the Turkish Communist Party.

Now, a few weeks later, I catch sight of the red-hammer-and-gear banner of the TKP fluttering among a sea of rainbow flags as we approach the broad wrought iron gates of Galatasaray Lisesi. The police presence thickens. Their armored cars, mounted with water cannons, line the Istiklal, forcing protestors into a choke point. The marchers stop. Excited Turkish youths weave in and out of the crowd, their faces covered with rainbow neckerchiefs in a Billy the Kid bandit style. From the storefronts, onlookers take photos. A woman elbows past me, her face veiled in the niqab. Her husband follows behind, wearing the long, two-fist beard of a Salafist. She pulls an iPad from her Louis Vuitton bag. Raising it up, she takes photos of the drag queens.

Encountering so many police, the protest organizers who've marched at the crowd's front sit down, blocking the road. Still clutching their rainbow flag, they begin to chant "Everywhere is revolution!" and "The government murders kids!"—a reference to Berkin Elvan, a fifteen-year-old who was killed when police fired a teargas canister that hit him in the head during Gezi. While police look on, a throng of women and transgender women release a shrill bedouin wail, which echoes along the Istiklal. Peeking into the armored trucks, I glimpse the officers sitting up, alert. The protestors glance back, watching them. From the armored turrets, a few water cannons rotate on their swivels, taking aim.

Gezi's memory is visceral here: after the government ordered the first protest encampment scuttled, transgender women fought side by side at the barricades among the initial activists. As Vince, Nate, and I watch the water cannons train their barrels on the march's transgender ringleaders, a British journalist hears us speaking in English. "The toughest men at Gezi," he informs us, "were the transgender women."

After another hour, we decide to grab dinner at a kebab stand off the Istiklal. As we slide out of the protest, it maintains a festive air despite the tension from moments before. It seems good and right to see so many disparate groups coming out to support a single, disenfranchised voice.

As we turn to go, something catches my eye. In the back of the crowd, mixing with the rainbow flags, and just a little larger, an anarchist flies a black banner.

⸺

Living in Istanbul, I am seven hours ahead of Eastern Standard Time, so I often find myself up in the night checking emails that are sent end of day in the United States and reading headlines on my phone. Just past midnight on my June 1, news breaks that the Taliban have released American prisoner of war Sergeant Bowe Bergdahl. I skim the story, and then I check my email. There's a message from Nate: "So, I was in Bowe Bergdahl's unit when he deserted."

I ask if he's got a minute to talk on the phone.

There were many stories about how Bowe Bergdahl was captured. In one video released by the Taliban, Bergdahl said he had lagged behind on a patrol and been taken. For years, it stood as a kind of accusation against his comrades: they had left him behind. But on the day Bergdahl disappeared, June 30, 2009, there was in fact no patrol, according to other soldiers who were there. Some of the men in his unit—Second Platoon, Blackfoot Company—still seem unable to forgive him for this fact. On that night, instead of patrolling, they slept in the earthen bunkers of OP Mest, an outpost scraped from a hillside in Afghanistan's rugged and remote Paktika Province. Life at OP Mest had been miserable: weeklong rotations in the scorching heat, no showers, no food except for MREs.

The next morning, Sergeant First Class Larry Hein took muster. Then the misery really began. Bergdahl was gone. Most of his equipment—rifle, helmet, body armor—had been left behind. He'd taken his camera, diary, and compass. The platoon fanned out, desperately searching for him. Earlier that morning, he had asked his team leader whether it would cause problems if he left base with his equipment. The team leader told Bergdahl that if he took his rifle or night-vision goggles, it would indeed cause problems. At nine a.m., Hein called over the radio to report a missing soldier. Bergdahl was then classified DUSTWUN—Duty Status: Whereabouts Unknown.

A little before five p.m. that afternoon, Colonel Michael Howard, the senior officer responsible for Paktika as well as two other eastern provinces, ordered that "all operations will cease until the missing soldier is found. All assets will be focused on the DUSTWUN situation and sustainment operations." That directive, as powerful as the word of God, changed Blackfoot Company's war. Recovering Bowe Bergdahl became a central mission.

That night on the phone, Nate tells me how "a human wave of insurgents" surprised an outpost at Zerok, in eastern Paktika Province, a few days after Bergdahl disappeared. Two Americans from the 3rd Battalion, 509th Infantry, were killed; many more were wounded. The soldiers at Zerok were more vulnerable than they otherwise would have been because there was a reduced complement of drones and intelligence aircraft available. These assets had been diverted to assist in the search for Bergdahl. Beginning that August, Nate noted how the 1st Battalion, 501st Infantry—Bergdahl's battalion—lost six soldiers in a three-week period. Morris Walker, Clayton Bowen, Kurt Curtiss, Darryn Andrews, Matthew Martinek, Michael Murphrey—each of these fatalities occurred on a mission that was related to, or influenced by, the effort to find Bergdahl.

In this remote part of an increasingly remote war, suffering and loss, the senselessness of Afghanistan, often played out in Bergdahl's name. By March 2010, Bergdahl's infantry battalion had returned home without him. Before they left, the army mandated they sign nondisclosure agreements. Bergdahl's story wouldn't be theirs to tell.

———

I served as a special operations officer in Paktika for a good part of 2010 and 2011, working out of a remote firebase a little more than a mile from the Pakistani border. At night we'd climb on our bunkered roof, a tumbler of scotch or cigar in hand, and watch the drone strikes in South Waziristan. During those days, Bergdahl's case loomed ever-present in much of our work. Like a chimera, he seemed just out of grasp. The irony that an iconic figure in a war that had largely been deserted by the American people was probably a deserter himself was never lost on us. It seemed just our luck.

Among sailors, a crew member who brings bad luck is known as a Jonah. It's a long-held superstition. And like the hapless crew that sailed

Jonah to Tarshish, we found ourselves in a storm. Imaginations ran wild. How did the Taliban in Paktika execute attacks with such unusual precision and lethality? Some hypothesized that Bergdahl had informed them of our tactics. Why did Afghan civilians refuse needed civil aid, becoming hostile? Others believed rumors that Bergdahl had participated in a propaganda campaign against us. None of this could be substantiated, but over there Bergdahl became the idol of discontent for so many. He was the Jonah.

And this wasn't only among the rank and file. One of my colleagues, a CIA case officer, had the collateral duty of collecting information on Bergdahl's whereabouts. For months, his location was known with a high degree of precision. Certain options had been floated as to what a recovery mission might look like. After flying in and out of Kabul for endless rounds of interagency meetings, my colleague grew frustrated by the army's inaction when provided with information by CIA. Then a senior military officer pulled him aside. "No one's serious about a rescue mission," he said. "It'd be too risky. Maybe if Bergdahl had actually been captured they'd do something, but he deserted."

My colleague flew back to our firebase and returned to his desk. He continued to track Bergdahl, cursing him all the while. Bergdahl became the idol of his discontent also. His Jonah.

———

During my eight-year military career, I only met one deserter. It was early in 2003, and I was fresh out of college, a newly minted second lieutenant on my way to Iraq. At Marine Corps Base Quantico, where I underwent training, we had to get decals for our cars from the provost marshall's office, the base cops. Behind a counter, stamping an endless ream of forms, stood a man in his early sixties. He was silver-haired, with a ruddy alcoholic's complexion. He wore the same MARPAT camouflage utilities as me, but his shirt's tapered cut bulged where age ran his stomach to fat. On his collar, he wore no rank. He was a private. As he stamped my form, I couldn't stop looking at him. He didn't seem to mind. I'm sure I wasn't the first. We exchanged pleasantries. I can't remember much of what we said, but I remember when he called me "Sir." The way he smiled when he said it.

Later I learned that the sixty-year-old private deserted during the Vietnam War. He'd gone to Canada and reentered the country some years later. In 1977, on his first day in office, President Carter pardoned those who avoided the draft as well as military deserters who had not yet been convicted or punished, but individuals were still required to apply for clemency. During the Iraq War, the Marine Corps had opened dozens of long-cold desertion cases, sending a message to my generation as it headed to war. The old private I met had seen this renewed effort and turned himself in. Offered a brief stint in the brig and a fine, he finished out his enlistment instead.

And that's what I remember about his smile: he seemed to recognize both the sanctity and absurdity of his choice.

———

Among veterans of the Afghanistan War, Bergdahl's return unleashes a torrent of emotion, much of it vitriolic. For many, he continues to be an idol of discontent, the Jonah of our Afghan voyage. For others, he's a different type of idol, the POW brought home with a hero's trappings. In a conflict that eschews war's traditional definitions of front lines, combatants, and armies, it's difficult to define what he has become. Over five years of captivity, Bowe Bergdahl was, more than anything else, a symbol, used by many: his former comrades, the Taliban, and the White House, which revealed the details of the prisoner swap a few days after President Obama's speech announcing a 2016 withdrawal from Afghanistan, a deadline that would soon lapse like the many set before it.

After the announcement of Bergdahl's release, a former soldier from his squad in Blackfoot Company immediately sends out his recollections of the disappearance in more than one hundred tweets. He concludes by writing: "So without B going missing we wouldn't have been in certain places. And without being in those places, 2 brothers wouldn't have given the ultimate sacrifice. They went out like fucking Hero's." A few tweets later, referring to his nondisclosure agreement, he writes: "Anybody got a lawyer btw?"

The night the news breaks, Nate and I speak for nearly three hours. Just before we hang up, he puts it more succinctly: "He's back and my friends are still dead."

The only clear thing in any of this is the suffering. For five years, Bergdahl suffered as an idol. The soldiers sent to recover that idol suffered too. Each was affected by Bergdahl's disappearance, and each will decide whether he wishes to forgive Bergdahl—or whether he will continue to be their Jonah.

That story had its end also. After being thrown overboard by his shipmates and swallowed by the whale, Jonah prayed to God:

When my soul fainted within me

I remembered the Lord. . . .

Those who regard worthless idols

forsake their own mercy. . . .

So the Lord spoke to the fish, and it vomited Jonah onto dry land.

THE SULEIMANI PHOTOGRAPH

AMIRLI

I wonder if Abu Bakr al-Baghdadi reads Mao?

This is what I am thinking as I sit in my Istanbul flat when the first news of a blitzkrieg next door in northern Iraq comes across the wires. It is late June and the streets are lazy with heat. The Turks have emptied their city, abandoning it to the advance of sweltering temperatures. In Haditha, Samarra, Tikrit, the Iraqi residents abandon their cities as well. After a handful of days, the Islamic State seizes the Mosul Dam. They threaten thousands of Yezidi families with extermination in the Sinjar Mountains. They are poised just outside the Kurdish capital of Erbil. It seems as if al-Baghdadi has ripped a page out of Mao's classic 1937 treatise *On Guerrilla Warfare*.

Mao Zedong wrote the book at the outset of the Second Sino-Japanese War, when Japan invaded the Chinese mainland. It was an argument for a new type of struggle, one that he and the Chinese Communists successfully waged for the next eight years. It lays out what has since become widely accepted as the three-phase Maoist model, the sine qua non of an effective insurgency.

In phase one, the guerrillas earn the population's support by distributing propaganda and attacking the organs of government. In phase two, escalating attacks are launched against the government's military forces and vital institutions. And in phase three, conventional warfare and fighting are used to seize cities, overthrow the government, and assume control of the country.

The Islamic State's advance leaves America's military and political leaders reeling, even though we are quite familiar with the three-phase Maoist model—it was used to great effect against us over the course of the Vietnam War. Ho Chi Minh adhered to this strategy, and even after he took ill in 1960 and died in 1969, his successor, Lê Duẩn, followed it, culminating in the 1975 Spring Offensive, when columns of North Vietnamese regulars, riding in Chinese-made tanks, invaded South Vietnam, leading to the eventual fall of Saigon.

During a summer of offensives and counteroffensives, the Islamic State's columns of captured American Humvees and tanks pace the desert in a war of maneuver. This language of advance and retreat, ground seized, sieges laid, bears closer resemblance to the Second World War than the quagmire of Iraq's long-running insurgency. Among America's leadership, confusion sets in. President Obama appears on television and, ridiculed for wearing a khaki summer suit, as if he didn't plan to face the cameras that day, concedes that his administration does not yet have a strategy to combat the Islamic State. He calls them "terrorists." No doubt their tactics have been barbaric—mass executions, the beheading of journalists during this same summer—but words matter, and to refer to them simply as terrorists negates their very serious political goals.

The West continues to refer to the Islamic State as ISIL or ISIS, refusing to align its vision of these radicals with the vision they hold of themselves: as a state. Does refusing to acknowledge their vision help us defeat the Islamic State? A less than nuanced understanding of the adversary was one of our great strategic blunders during Vietnam. While American policy makers spoke about "domino theory" and "rolling back communism," their North Vietnamese counterparts spoke largely in terms of national unity and a long history of intervention and oppression by foreign powers—the Chinese included, despite Mao's intellectual influence on Ho Chi Minh.

July swelters on as an ever-expanding inkblot of Islamic State conquests spreads across the Iraqi provinces of al-Anbar, Nineveh, others. Erbil remains under threat, with fighting in its suburbs of Makmour and Gwer. Both towns fall but are retaken by Kurdish peshmerga fighters, whose name translates as "those who face death." And the unthinkable—that Baghdad could fall—seems possible. Both American and Iranian advisers flood into that city, for it's not hard to imagine that the Islamic State's summer offensive of 2014 could be similar in scope to North Vietnam's spring offensive of 1975. It seems phase three of Mao's treatise, conventional warfare, is well underway.

As for phases one and two, those were the American war in Iraq.

Even back when Abu Musab al-Zarqawi was leading al-Qaeda in Mesopotamia nearly a decade ago, the organization's aim was the establishment of an Islamic state. Its courtship of Sunni tribal leaders and ex-Ba'athists in the wake of the American-led invasion adhered to Mao's idea of phase one operations, and the full-scale insurgency beginning in 2004 also fit within the Maoist construct of phase two operations.

So maybe Abu Bakr al-Baghdadi (or Caliph Ibrahim) is reading *On Guerrilla Warfare*, or maybe he's not, but what seems clear is that he's got a strategy, one adhering to a method that has worked in the past, one that's facilitated the founding of nations, regardless of whether those nations conform to international norms of human rights and basic decency.

The American response grows: an airdrop of humanitarian supplies to the trapped Yezidis in the Sinjar Mountains, limited air strikes that expand as limited air strikes always do, and military advisers. We return to war as we promise we are not returning to war. By August, President Obama announces to the country, "As commander in chief, I will not allow the United States to be dragged into fighting another war in Iraq. And so even as we support Iraqis as they take the fight to these terrorists, American combat troops will not be returning to fight in Iraq."

Define *combat troops*? The pilots on their bombing runs are not combat troops. The military advisers embedded within the crumbling Iraqi Army are not combat troops. Who will do the fighting? A strange alliance begins to coalesce, old adversaries forced into coalition. They will fight the Islamic State in a place called Amirli.

Wars often end with an iconic image: Lee and Grant at Appomattox Court House, the Japanese surrendering aboard the USS *Missouri*, a helicopter lifting off the CIA station's roof in Saigon. Over the summer, images begin to trickle out of Amirli, a town of twenty thousand Shiite-Turkmen in Saladin Province. Machine-gun-wielding militiamen. Columns of smoke curling among palm groves. Homes crushed to dust in streets of dust. On my phone, on my laptop, there is no shortage of such images. As I wonder if one might signal the end of the Iraq War, I find myself looking at the photo that marked its beginning, for me.

The picture that I have from the war's beginning was taken in late May 2003, on the day I was commissioned as a second lieutenant. It shows me with my friend and mentor Douglas Zembiec, the Marine major who ran my special operations training. The two of us are in Boston, on the deck of the USS *Constitution*, the oldest commissioned warship in the US Navy. Standing between the masts, we wear our dress blues, with their antiquated high collars and brass buttons. Doug has just pinned my bars on my epaulettes. We're both smiling. I look proud, and he proud of me.

The photo was taken about three weeks after President Bush's "Mission Accomplished" speech. We'd missed the opening salvos of the invasion, but within eighteen months Doug would fight in the First Battle of Fallujah and I would fight in the Second. Both of us would be wounded. Doug was decorated for his valor, and a much-circulated profile of him ran in the *Los Angeles Times*, headlined "The Unapologetic Warrior." When he was asked about the intense fighting he'd seen in April 2004, he replied with characteristic bombast: "I've told [my troops] that killing is not wrong if it's for a purpose, if it's to keep your nation free or to protect your buddy. One of the most noble things you can do is kill the enemy." Doug was always saying unfashionable things like that, and he believed them. I'd anchored myself in his mentorship because of his unshakable faith in being a Marine. The years of combat to follow made more sense when you held on to those kinds of precepts, when they felt true.

Doug returned from Iraq to Camp Pendleton, California, that fall. While he was home, his first child, a daughter, was born. He was eventually detailed to CIA, which deployed him to Baghdad as an adviser to an Iraqi counterterrorism unit. The Quds Force, a special forces unit of Iran's elite Revolutionary Guards, was extremely active in Iraq at the time, providing guidance and equipment to the Shiite insurgency there. The head of the Quds Force, General Qassem Suleimani, was orchestrating a proxy war against the US and Iraqi governments using several Shiite militias as surrogates.

On the night of May 11, 2007, Doug led an Iraqi squad on a raid against the Mahdi Army, a Shiite militia operating in Sadr City. As he rushed down an alley, with several soldiers behind him, he was hit by a burst of machine gun fire beneath the eye and instantly killed. The Iraqi soldiers evacuated his body, calling over the radio, "Five wounded and one martyred."

The word *martyred* implies sacrifice for a purpose. It recalls for me Doug's words in the *Los Angeles Times*. Accounts from that night describe Doug spotting militia fighters as they set up a machine gun, then pushing several of his men out of the way, saving their lives. For years, when I remembered Doug, this act had seemed purpose enough, and the Marine Corps revered him for the sacrifice too. His funeral, at the Naval Academy Chapel, in Annapolis, was Homeric in scale, and the Corps named buildings and awards after him. At Baghdad International Airport, in 2008, General David Petraeus, the commander of coalition forces in Iraq at the time, dedicated a helicopter landing zone in his honor.

I've often felt the urge, looking at the picture of the two of us from

2003, to pair it with another one, as if to bookend the war and that period of my life. If, during this time when wars seem to lack a defined end, I could not have a Lee at Appomattox or a surrender on the deck of a battleship, perhaps I might make a separate peace. Then in August, scrolling through images coming from Amirli, I find the photo I am after.

For six weeks, with food, water, and medical supplies dwindling, and armed with little more than rifles, Amirli's Shiite Turkmen have held out against the Islamic State. A relief force has fought in three directions to reach them: the Iraqi Army from the south, Kurdish peshmerga from the north, and Shiite militiamen, to include Iranian-backed militias, such as the Badr Corps and Asa'ib Ahl al-Haq along with Quds Force advisers, from the east. The aircraft of two nations fly overhead: Iranian surveillance drones and American close air support and humanitarian aid sorties. The picture I find, which appears to have been first posted online by Digital Resistance, an alternative news website, was taken on the outskirts of Amirli. In the center of the frame, wearing brown trousers, a beige baseball cap, and a keffiyeh, stands a man I recognize as General Suleimani, the head of the Quds Force. He isn't quite smiling, but he looks pleased. Flanking him is an unidentified Iraqi soldier wearing a green T-shirt with "ARMY" printed on it and carrying an American-issue M4 carbine slung across his chest. With their Iranian advisers and matériel, and with the surveillance drones launched from Baghdad International Airport, the Shiite militias had achieved a significant victory in Amirli.

When I look at the photo, I can't help but think that Suleimani would recognize the irony that his victory was due in part to the very

US air power that his surrogates had once dodged in Sadr City, where Doug was killed. I doubt he would be aware of a further irony: that his surveillance drones were taking off right next to Zembiec Landing Zone. Given that wars are no longer punctuated by clear declarations of victory or defeat, the photo seems an appropriate bookend, concluding one memory of Iraq so that another might begin.

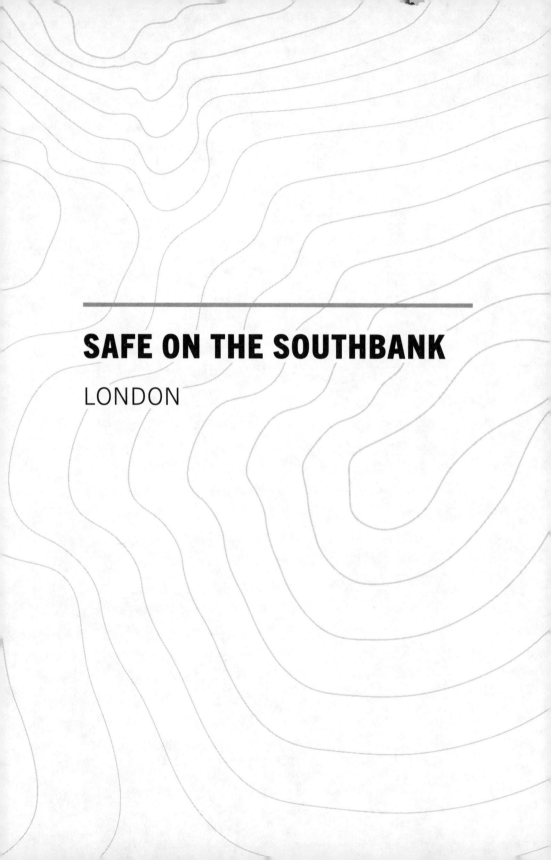

SAFE ON THE SOUTHBANK

LONDON

The same summer as Amirli, on the way back to the United States for a visit, I pass through London, where I grew up. I often find an excuse to return, for unimportant reasons, just to wander the city when I get the chance. It's a habit that began after I'd finished my first tour in Iraq, when after the Fallujah battle my parents offered to treat me to a vacation as a Christmas gift, anywhere I wanted to go. When I said London, they seemed a bit surprised. Why not choose a more exotic destination, one that was less familiar to me? I told them that after seven months in the desert, I wanted to be somewhere cold and wet. At the time this made sense, but a decade later I've realized I wanted to return for a different reason: Southbank.

When I was nine, we packed up our home in Los Angeles and arrived at Heathrow on a gray January morning. My financier father had taken a job running his firm's London office. My mother, a novelist, quickly settled into the city's vibrant literary scene. My brother, a gifted mathematician at only eleven, skipped a grade, excelling in our new school. But without my beloved beaches and endless blue-sky days, I floundered. Until I made a discovery.

Southbank, at an eastern bend in the Thames, is the epicenter of British skateboarding. Sheltered from London's incessant rain by an undercroft, the space has stairs, ledges, and a large, smoothly paved expanse that sweeps into a three-sided bank. Graffiti artists worked there unmolested, homeless people slept in the corners, the sidewalk smelled faintly of urine, and the continuous crashing of skateboards left your head ringing. I loved it.

I soon made friends with the local skaters: Big Clive, a Jamaican kid from Brixton; Toby Shuall, the son of an Israeli jeweler; James "Paddy" Neasdon, whose uncle may have been in the IRA. I became "Fat Yank"—the lean Marine with the buzz cut coming later. We spoke our own language. Skateboarding tricks: *backside tailslide, varial kickflip.* Girls: *She's a total Bettie.* Put-downs: *Don't be a T-Dog, land the trick.* And my favorite: *safe.*

Safe meant "cool." It meant "hello." It meant "don't worry about it." Once, when trying a certain trick on the beam, a long wooden ledge topped with shards of granite, I toppled onto the stones, damaging a nerve in my hand—my right index finger still tingles when it's cold out—and Toby came over, helping me up. "Safe, man. Safe." A few minutes later, when I landed the trick, my friends banged their boards on the ground, shouting, "Safe! Safe! Safe!" And that's what mattered—landing tricks, being a good skater.

When I was fifteen, my family moved to Washington, D.C. I tried skateboarding there, but the locals were far less welcoming. Within a couple of years, I'd given it up. It was time to start thinking about college, the future. My parents were surprised when I decided to join the Marines, but the draw soon became obvious. The insider language: *The enemy's TTP is to use frags.* The varied backgrounds: my first platoon had kids from Texas, the Dominican Republic, and Canada within its ranks. And the importance of being good—or as Marines say, tactically competent.

Over eight years, friends like Staff Sergeant Sean "the Skwerl" Brownlee and Gunnery Sergeant Willy "Bare Knuckles" Parent became dear comrades, replacements for my skater friends. Other friends I lost: Dan Malcom, Garrett "Tubes" Lawton, J.P. Blecksmith, Paul Fellsberg, Aaron Torian—a roll call of ghosts who follow me still.

When I returned to London after my Iraq deployment in 2004, I found myself wandering down to Southbank, spending hours there. I've returned several times since, as I do in the weeks after Amirli.

The day is cold but clear. Tourists and Londoners stop to watch the skaters. I mix among the onlookers but want to get closer. Weaving among the kids who rush by on their boards, I find my way to the beam. I sit on the petrified piece of wood and run my hands along the shards of granite cemented to its top. I can still feel the tingling in my finger, the one I've stopped thinking of as my right index finger and have, some years before, started thinking of as my trigger finger.

Then a rail-thin teenager, in a baggy white T-shirt badly in need of a wash, skids up to the beam. He sits next to me, reaching into his pocket for an envelope of tobacco. He seems not to notice the geezer perched next to him. But soon I catch a few of his wary glances.

"I was a local here twenty years ago," I tell him.

He licks down the paper of his hand-rolled cigarette. Then, slowly, he begins to nod his head. "Safe, man. Safe."

"Yeah," I say. "Safe."

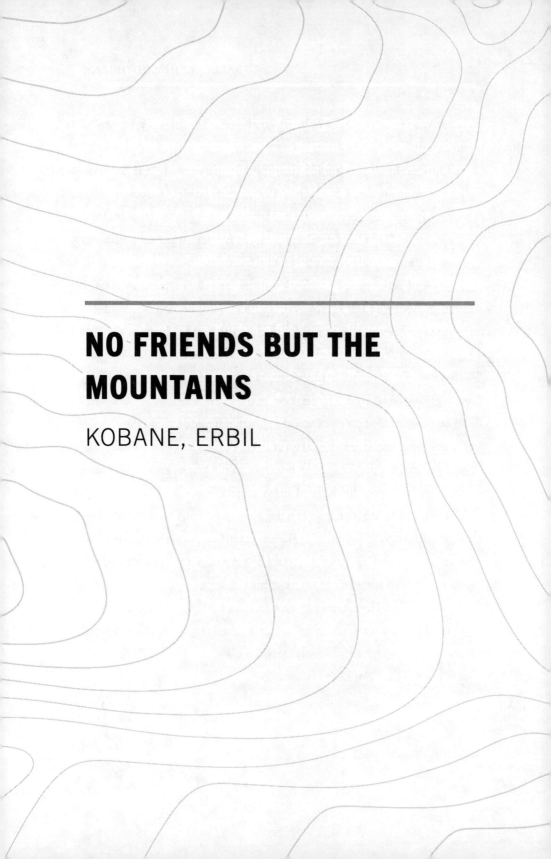

NO FRIENDS BUT THE MOUNTAINS

KOBANE, ERBIL

I t is autumn now, a few weeks before Thanksgiving of 2014. In a farm field outside of Kobane, the slick mud freezes into sludgy clods, which threaten to clog the tire wells of the black Peugeot we drive everywhere. The horizon has condensed into a dark mass, a mix of slate clouds and cement buildings, their tops shorn at jagged angles from the weeks-long battle. We arrived that morning from Gaziantep, on our way into northern Iraq, just Matt and me. Some of Matt's clients have expressed an interest in the humanitarian fallout from the Islamic State's siege of Kobane, the most significant engagement since the fighting around Amirli, so he thinks it'll be useful to take a quick detour here, to see what's what. I just want to see it. A few days before, Matt had visited Kobane with a journalist who'd flown in to write a piece about the battle at this strategic border crossing. The two of them had watched US air strikes from a hilltop barely inside of Turkey. When too many journalists gathered, the Turkish authorities had dispersed the crowd with CS gas. This morning, those same Turkish authorities won't allow us past their checkpoint on the D833, the main thoroughfare into the city. So we drive across the farm field.

Our Peugeot's axle crunches against frozen troughs of earth, the noise like teeth on hard candy. To break an axle out here falls into the category of unimaginable. A flat tire, only slightly less so. We check behind us, toward the D833, which soon dissolves on our rear horizon. We're looking for a way around the Turkish checkpoints so we might get to the hill where Matt had watched the air strikes. He points out a dirt road that threads between two fields. We ease in that direction, again scraping against the troughs. Though we hardly exceed ten miles per hour, it is a white-knuckle drive as we pray our car won't break down.

It seems appropriate that Matt and I should crawl toward the Islamic State's siege of Kobane, for its columns have slowed to a crawl as well, stalling here after a summer of blitzkrieg. The name Kobane isn't native to the region: it comes from the German word *kompanie*, after the railway company whose workers built the town in tandem with a section of the Konya-Baghdad Railway in 1911. That this obscure backwater might prove to be the high-water mark of the Islamic State's advance is no less remarkable than the fact that those who will stop them are, until recently, an equally obscure people: the Kurds.

There is a saying among them: *We have no friends but the mountains.*

The Kurds of Iraq, Syria, Turkey, and Iran have a long tradition of retreating into the mountains of their native lands to wage insurgency. When Kurdish men or women leave home to join any number of separatist groups—the PKK, YPG, PJAK, PUK—it is said they are *going to the mountains.*

With the rise of the Islamic State, the Western powers need the Kurds to come down from the mountains, to provide the ground troops that the Americans, British, French, and others are loathe to commit.

Matt has a history of working alongside the Kurds. Shortly after graduating college in Boston, he took a position at the American University of Iraq in Sulaimani. The school was a novelty then, largely financed and supported by Dr. Barham Salih, a bookish and bespectacled former Patriotic Union of Kurdistan dissident who in 2006, when Matt arrived, had ascended to the office of deputy prime minister of Iraq. In those early days, a cluster of trailers composed the university's campus while a handful of students toiled away at their degrees, dreaming of the time when they might ascend to membership of Iraq's—or even an independent Kurdistan's—educated elite. With long-held national ambitions, the Kurds have used the last decade of chaos among Arab-Iraqis to consolidate power, creating the Kurdistan Regional Government, or KRG, which administers an autonomous zone in the north.

Today the American University of Iraq in Sulaimani encompasses several hundred acres of glass and sandstone buildings. Filled with the trappings of any major Western university, the simple existence of such a place challenges certain of my conceptions: this is not the Iraq I knew, one of cratered streets and crumbling buildings with little prospect of repair, one of idle men watching our foot patrols with hard stares. The country is different in the north. As Dr. Barham is fond of pointing out, "Though the Iraq War did not turn out well for you Americans, I am a single-issue voter. Any Kurd who dreams of their own nation will forever be indebted to George W. Bush's freedom agenda."

Yet the most costly gifts are those given for free. With the rise of the Islamic State, the Kurds must now spill blood to hold on to their last decade of gains. Their neighbors to the northwest, the Turks, are leery, if not openly hostile, to Western collusion with the Kurds in the fight against the Islamic State.

Matt and I continue to cross the rutted farm field, stumbling upon

a wisp of dirt road that takes us far around the checkpoint we'd en-
countered on the D833, and it seems we'll be able to loop back toward
Kobane and find our way to the hilltop. But before we can upshift from
first to second gear, we turn a bend that leads us into a serpentine of
concertina wire obstructed by an armored car on the far side. There is
no time to change course. We brake on the shoulder, just before the
wire. A pair of Turkish soldiers hops out of the cab, striding toward us,
rifles leveled, hands riding pistol grips and barrels. Matt raises his
palms from the steering wheel, presenting them toward the windshield.
I do the same. It's been some time since I've been eye to eye with a teenage soldier. A young man who has yet to shave, carrying a gun, holds a
unique type of menace: inexperience and unaccountability often go
hand in hand. When one of the soldiers noses the barrel of his rifle up
the road, so we might go back to where we came, we turn around and
give up on Kobane.

We head east instead, farther into the mountains, and at a place
called Silopi we'll cross into Iraq.

———

For five hours we drive in fifth gear, tracing the border. A mesh and wire
fence oscillates toward and then away from us, coming so close that at
times I could throw the can of Diet Coke I'm sipping into Syria, or the
part of Syria that is now called the Islamic State. At other times the
fence recedes into the distance, nearly disappearing, only to sweep
back toward our car, as if it might run us off the road. Less than an hour
from the crossing, the border juts north, then hooks back down, following the Dicle Nehri, a tributary of the Tigris, which—along with its

cousin, the Euphrates—makes the vast desert south of us something more: Mesopotamia, the "Land of the Two Rivers."

We are driving into Silopi now. Buildings crowd the choked roads, their half dozen or so floors stacking unevenly upward, leaning over us, as if their balconies wished to clasp onto one another in friendship, like the Damascene homes in Abed's poem. Our papers are in order, but the authorities' byzantine shuffling of permissions and visas will take hours, so Matt and I pull over to grab a late lunch, knowing it'll be some time before we eat again. We park the Peugeot with two of its four tires on the sidewalk, which is the practice here, and wander into a kebab shop that looks like any other: a window display like a butcher's, space heaters buzzing inside, a lazy cluster of men sipping tea. The tiled floor gleams while flies orbit the meat. We place our order and sit. Before cooking our meal, the owner, a man who looks as if he developed his frown, stubble, and thick mustache in utero, makes a point of turning up the volume on two televisions. Their songs drown one another out, but the programming he plays for us needs no translation: a choir of women stand in a green, flowered field. They wear a traditional pastiche of brightly colored gowns: yellow, pink, blue. Behind them, men dressed like Bible salesmen, in black slacks and white shirts, play their instruments: hand drums, lutes, wooden guitars. The song has a swinging cadence, one that's easy to march to. Snaps of fighting cut in and out of the frame: a heavy machine gun on the back of a pickup truck chugs out egg-shaped bullets, men charge through a field that isn't grass but dirt, women march with Kalashnikov rifles slung tightly across their chests the way Western women might wear a BabyBjörn. There's only one word I understand in the lyrics, repeated in a loop that gains force with repetition: *Kobane! Kobane! Kobane!*

While I watch the televisions, Matt makes two calls. The first is to a Turkish contact who will drop us at the border and then look after the Peugeot while we are in Iraq. The second is to Dara, a Kurdish alumnus of the American University whom Matt hasn't seen in six years. Once in Iraq, Dara will give us a ride to Erbil. With the afternoon listing toward evening, we finish our kebabs, pay the bill, and wander outside. The armored cars of the Turkish gendarmes flit back and forth, mingling with and at times cleaving through the traffic. Although the Kurdish motorists yield to them, behind each windshield there is a scowl, one that's familiar to me. When driving in a column of armored Humvees in Iraq, I saw the same look from the motorists who yielded the road to us.

Matt's Turkish contact soon arrives and drops us at the border. As our Peugeot speeds away, I wonder if we'll ever see it again. Matt seems unconcerned. It's a confidence that comes from having been stranded before, as a researcher in Iraq and Afghanistan, as a journalist in North Africa, as a student in Lebanon. His optimism is not rooted in the certainty that nothing will happen but rather that if something does happen, he'll be able to figure out what to do next.

"I guess we should find somebody to show our passports to," he says, as we amble along the highway's shoulder. Parked next to us, and extending for hundreds of yards, is a line of cargo-laden sixteen-wheelers. None are moving. Many appear abandoned by their drivers. This seems to be a trip that is not easily completed. I'd assumed Matt had made this overland crossing before, but I realize now that he hasn't. So I tell myself we'll figure it out as we go, attempting to mimic his optimism.

A van pulls up next to us. The driver, a teenage boy with a shaggy bowl cut and threadbare sports coat, can't stop looking at Matt, seemingly entranced by this six-foot-plus, blond-haired, blue-eyed giant who has appeared at his border crossing. Circling toward us from the passenger door comes an older man. His features—a ridged nose, jutting lips, and fleshy cheeks that sag—are of an imprecise composition, like the work of an unskilled sculptor, and when looking at him I can see the ugliness that the boy will grow into and I realize the two are of some relation. The older man reaches for my bag and I jerk away. His mouth cinches into a frown, which he overcomes. "Forty lira," he says, raising his smile like a flag of truce and pointing into Iraq.

Matt and I look up toward the border crossing, a bridge that spans a flooded marsh. Mixing among the zigzag of checkpoints and obstacles are a couple of vans similar to this man's, and it seems he will facilitate our passage with the customs authorities. And the amount he demands is nothing.

"Forty lira?" asks Matt, expecting to pay more.

The man and the boy exchange a quick look. They are partners just as Matt and I are, even down to their matching sports coats, the chauffer's uniform they seem to have agreed upon.

"Thirty-five," the man answers.

Matt laughs, offering his hand.

The man takes our bags and loads them into the back. Then he opens the van's sliding door, sweeping his hand inside with a flourish. As we pull into a queue of trucks, cars, and other vans, he offers us bottled water and breath mints. He turns on the heater, holding his thick, stubby fingers in front of the vent while glancing back at us to make sure we are neither too warm nor too cold. He seems quite intent on our comfort, and while we wait for an audience with the Turkish and then the Iraqi gendarmes, the man and the boy sit rigidly in the front seat and vacantly stare through the windshield. One will say something, a minute or two will pass, then the other will reply. In this way they extend what would be an hour's conversation into a day's worth. The intimacy of slow conversation is one I know well, and the cadence of their exchange reminds me of days spent on patrol in a Humvee with Ames, or Pratt, or any number of Marines who were my friends. This crossing into Iraq marks ten years to the day since Dan Malcom was killed on the high-rise. It is also my first time back since the war. Yet when I mentioned this anniversary to Matt, it rings with hollow significance for me, perhaps because not enough time has passed. If I were to return twenty or thirty years later, maybe the experience would feel equal to the catharsis of D-Day veterans who've walked the placid beaches of Normandy or Vietnam veterans who have wandered the lush, verdant jungle north of Saigon. Returning to the country where I fought my war, while that country is still at war, offers no closure. It does not end an experience, but only adds to it. And if what I am doing is additive, then my war is not over.

We navigate the first Turkish checkpoint with little trouble. The older man simply takes our passports, visas, and residency cards and disappears into a nondescript trailer on the bridge's near side for the better part of an hour. When he returns, the gendarme who accompanies him knocks on the van's side window, waking both the boy, who has fallen asleep behind the wheel, and Matt and me in the back seat. The gendarme glances at us, then our passports, and waves us all across. We pass a candy-striped gate, weave through some Jersey barriers, and then, just ahead, I catch a glimpse of a tricolor banner—red, white, and green, with a yellow sun affixed to the center: the Kurdish flag. I search for an Iraqi one, but it seems they've stopped flying it. The late-afternoon sun is tangerine, and we're running out of light.

The van jars to a stop in no-man's-land.

The old man hops out, jogging across the road to a three-story building. "Where is he going?" I ask, mindful of the late hour. Before Matt can take a guess, the boy slides open the side door, motioning for us to get out. We reach for our bags, but he shakes his head as if that won't be necessary. Then, as the two of us stand on the street, the boy pulls a screwdriver from his pocket and gets to work. He levers open the van's plastic side-paneling, he yanks up every seat cushion, he unscrews the coverings along the wheel wells. Within three minutes, the boy has stripped open a dozen compartments. Just as Matt and I begin to understand what he's doing, his partner shuffles out of the building. Shopping bags filled with cartons of duty-free cigarettes hang from the older man's arms. He's even crammed a carton into each of the pockets of his sports coat. When he gets back to the van he fumbles half of the smokes over to the boy like a relay racer with too many batons, and the pair stuff their smuggled cargo into the many pried-open compartments. For the places where an entire carton won't fit, they tear open the boxes, tucking the packs of smokes between seat cushions, under floor mats, even pushing a pack into the foam padding of each headrest. With the van fully laden, the pair smile a weak apology at both Matt and me and offer us our now lumpy seats inside the van. The thirty-five lira we thought we paid to cross the border were really paid so we could serve as mules for this cigarette-smuggling operation.

When the sun finally sets, the older man is in another office with the Iraqi authorities, making his case for passage based on the strength of our US passports. By the time we cross the border, the Kurdish flag is invisible in the darkness. The boy parks the van on the road's dirt shoulder. To our south the stars peek above the jagged Qandil Mountains, a hint of light above the dark earth. On the other side of this range is Erbil. The older man circles around the van's front, helping Matt and me unload our bags. His courtesy arises not from his belief in servicing us as clients, but in his guilt at having roped us into his smuggling scheme. But what resentment can I feel toward someone who does what he must to survive?

So when the old man offers me a pack of smokes, I smile and take it. Little has changed here, and lighting the cigarette, I count out the ten years since I'd last had one in Iraq.

———

"Where are you, Dara?"

Matt cradles his cell phone to his ear. The wind has picked up, and his voice mixes with the roadside traffic and is nearly swept away.

"I'm right by the flagpole," Matt adds. "Which one? The huge fucking Kurdish one!" He laughs. "All right, see you in a second."

Whole schools of identical headlights rush past. I hope Dara finds us, because there is no way we'll find him. But before my anxieties can coalesce into actual concern, a black Audi Q6 parks next to us, kicking up a trail of dust that billows into my mouth. The SUV's door swings open and the cab's light spills into the street. A muscled Kurd with black, gelatinous hair and a white UFC "Tap Out" T-shirt barrels toward us. "Professor! You're so skinny!" he bellows at Matt, who is equally enormous, and the two embrace in a contortion that is half hug, half wrestling move. After a quick round of introductions, Dara tosses our bags into the back of the Audi. "Let's get going," he says. "Three hours to Dream City." I can only imagine he's referring to Erbil.

We pull out of Silopi, passing by a few Ford and Chevrolet dealerships, as well as two amusement parks replete with neon-lit Ferris wheels. While this procession of burgeoning Americana flits by my window, Matt and Dara cycle through a Rolodex of shared acquaintances, catching up on the last six years. "You didn't hear? He's in Germany." Or, "She's at the Ministry of Interior and doesn't return my calls." Dara is eager to query Matt about the faculty at the American University, making interjections like "We all thought he was a prick." Or, "Not once? Well, I thought you were sleeping with her." There is something universal in the conversation, the same as any student relishing an encounter with an old teacher, the two meeting as equals for the first time. Dara's phone interrupts them, its ringer set to the theme from *The Godfather*. In the quiet, I can hear annoyed staccato bursts of Kurdish through the receiver. Dara replies, equally annoyed. There is a brief argument and then he hangs up. "I didn't expect you guys to take so long," he says. "My mother's worried. She didn't want me to drive all the way out here. The last few months have been pretty bad."

The lights of Silopi disappear from the rearview as we snake our way into the Qandil Mountains, and I can feel the dark presence of the sheer ridges just off the road as Dara tells us about the fighting around Erbil and how in the summer many families evacuated. "Things are better now," he says, "but who knows. The Daesh are right outside of the city."

Our conversation ebbs to silence. The dark mountains untangle, spilling into a flat plain, its horizon pricked by flashes from the northern oil fields. The Kurds, unable to reach a deal with the government in

Baghdad, which heavily taxes its export barrels, now burn off their excess oil. Silhouetted by these fires, Erbil's jutting skyline comes into view, an entire city picketed by unfinished skyscrapers, the construction halted due to this oil dispute, the fight against the Islamic State, and the never-ending animus that seems to seep up from the ground in this part of the world. As we make our final approach to Dream City, Dara snatches his iPod from the glove box and plugs it into the Audi's ample sound system. "You like the Red-Headed Stranger?" he asks us.

"The who?" says Matt.

Before Dara can explain, Willie Nelson is well into the opening verses:

Mamas, don't let your babies grow up to be cowboys
Don't let 'em pick guitars and drive them old trucks
Make 'em be doctors and lawyers and such

Mamas, don't let your babies grow up to be cowboys
They'll never stay home and they're always alone
Even with someone they love

And as the peshmerga's first checkpoints come into view outside of Erbil, Dara and I are both singing while Matt, the Waspy New Englander, only hums along.

After Dara drops us at our hotel on Sixty Meter Road, a main boulevard in Erbil named after its width, we unload our bags from the back of his Audi. He then asks what neither Matt nor I have yet put words to: "So you guys want to go up to the front lines, right?" Sheepishly, we both nod.

After fighting in two wars with no front line, I want to see one, and I know Matt feels the same. The next morning Dara drives us to the Ministry of Peshmerga, where, after some coordination with a brigadier general, an audience is arranged for us with Staff Colonel Salim Surche, whose unit, the Erbil Battalion, is garrisoned in Makmour, a suburb southwest of town. We take our Audi to his headquarters, a youth sports center; it's a modern, three-story complex of steel and glass, its front drizzled with small-caliber bullet holes, as if someone had attacked it with a hole puncher. The Erbil Battalion reclaimed Makmour after the Islamic State seized the town for three days in September, nearly two months ago. Billeted in the complex, the peshmerga sleep between shifts on the line, burrowed beneath fleece blankets. Excited to see Americans, a few of them eagerly take us to a room upstairs, its windows shattered, dried blood crusting the tiled floor. They had killed two Islamic State fighters here weeks ago and never bothered to clean up the mess.

Over cigarettes and cups of spiced ginger tea in his office, Colonel Surche explains how the Islamic State captured Makmour, driving into town with eight armored Humvees. When I mention that this doesn't seem like a particularly large force to take an entire town, Colonel Surche's gaze retains its warmth even as his forehead knots, a thick single eyebrow splitting his face like a fraction line, one that divides the stern soldier from the hospitable man. "Perhaps if we had better weapons," he says, "this would be true, but what do we have? Only light machine guns. Our bullets bounce off their vehicles." He goes on to explain how the Islamic State has proved especially effective in regions with a Sunni Arab majority. "In these places," Colonel Surche says, "the population rises up with the militants, fighting alongside them." He then tells us to go see for ourselves, offering a HiLux pickup truck and six of his troopers as an escort.

We wind down a dirt road, arriving at the Erbil Battalion's forward-most positions with the Islamic State. I crouch behind a sandbagged berm and stare south, across nearly two kilometers of desert, at a cement factory, its cinder blocks pockmarked by gunfire. Sergeant Farhad Karzan, who is leading the eight other peshmerga fighters manning this position, hands me his binoculars. "If you watch long enough, you'll see them moving on the roof," he tells me. "But my binoculars don't work so well."

I lean against the parapet, my knees in the dirt. Next to me, Dara fingers through some tins of ammunition while Matt chats idly with a few of the junior soldiers. I lower my gaze into the binoculars. The right lens barely holds focus, and the left is cracked. Unable to see any movement along the front, I wait.

After a couple of minutes, one of the soldiers wanders over, apparently to get a better look at me, their visitor. He carries an M16A2, a rifle that the US military hasn't used widely for more than a decade. I rest the binoculars on the parapet, asking if I can see his rifle. He hands it to me, and I open the breech, sticking my pinky inside the firing chamber. It is immaculate, cleaner than I ever kept my rifle during my Marine days. Seeing that I know how to lock back the bolt on an M16A2 and inspect its mechanisms, Sergeant Karzan gives me a suspicious look, and I explain that I fought here a decade earlier. His entire face lights up. Reaching into his pants pocket, he removes a weathered ID card from the long-defunct Iraqi National Guard, dated back to 2004.

"Do you know my friend, Captain Luke?" he asks me. "We were in Mosul together." On the American-issued ID, a much younger version of Sergeant Karzan stares back at me, his head shaved, his face without its salt-and-pepper stubble.

I shake my head, no.

How could Sergeant Karzan think that I would know one American captain out of the thousands that had served in our eight-year war? But staring across the front, standing among the eight men at his position, the war seems a local, very personal affair. He then takes me over to a single PKM, a light machine gun of Soviet design. It rests on the parapet's corner, oriented toward the cement factory held by the Islamic State. "Aside from a few rifles, this is all we have to hold them back." Two cans of belted ammunition rest next to the gun, their links rusted. "Over there," says Sergeant Karzan, pointing to a smudge of upturned earth on the horizon, "is our other position. They have a machine gun too."

Rusted ammunition, eight peshmerga fighters, a tired old sergeant: this is the front line. An American carrier battle group flies sorties from the Persian Gulf. Drones orbit, unseen. But less than two kilometers from the Islamic State, it all evaporates—to nothing. Whether these peshmerga will stop the Islamic State's advance farther into Iraq *depends on that machine gun.* And I remember the William Carlos Williams poem that I, and so many other children, memorized in grammar school:

so much depends
upon

a red wheel
barrow

glazed with rain
water

beside the white
chickens

Sergeant Karzan offers me tea, but the escort that Colonel Surche has provided seems ready to depart. So we pile into their HiLux and say our goodbyes. Tearing down the road toward the Erbil Battalion's headquarters, I keep thinking about the gun pointed at the cement factory, and about that poem. This latest war in Iraq may well be decided by the smallest of things: a few men, a few guns, luck. Before visiting Sergeant Karzan's position, I had asked Colonel Surche what his orders were. He told me he had none, but that if the Ministry of Peshmerga ordered him to attack, he would, and they'd try to push the Islamic State back once more, until Kurdish forces reclaimed all the land they had lost over the summer and the fall.

When I get back to my hotel in Erbil that night, I look at a photograph I took of Sergeant Karzan's machine gun, and the expanse of desert stretching between his position and the Islamic State. I transcribe a few notes and then go to bed, the unrelenting traffic of Sixty Meter Road shuttling past my window, the drivers seemingly oblivious to the front line only thirty minutes away.

The next morning, Dara meets us for breakfast in the lobby. Before we can make a lap around the buffet, he grabs both Matt and me, showing us a news story in Kurdish on his phone. Just hours before, at first light, the Erbil Battalion attacked, advancing from their positions and taking the cement factory. Slowly, I graze over the buffet—fresh fruit, croissant, omelet—and sitting down with my coffee, I wonder how Sergeant Karzan and his eight men, and that one machine gun, have fared.

———

I've never visited the citadel of Erbil, and Matt insists it'd be a crime if I didn't see it. With the afternoon light quickly fading, we wander through souk Eskan. Beneath a catacomb of sandstone archways, Arab and Kurdish vendors hawk tailored suits, spices, and the latest iPhone from rickety shop fronts as we make our way to the ramparts. When I spot a baseball cap emblazoned with the Star of David, Matt explains that many Kurds have a strong affinity for Israel. Solidarity among minority groups antagonized by Arabs, he surmises. Outside the souk, mixing with the off-duty peshmerga who laze in sidewalk cafés, we spot several European aid workers and tourists smoking narghile and sipping chai. Then we pass a guard, half-asleep in his chair, and climb a large stone ramp to the citadel's portcullis.

Designated a UNESCO World Heritage Site just as the Islamic State swept into Mosul in June, the citadel of Erbil crowns a hillock in the city center. It is the world's oldest continually inhabited settlement, dating to the fifth millennium BC. Brick walls encircle the fortress, and for many Kurds it is a symbol of their resilience in the face of centuries of oppression. Residing within the walls is a city in miniature, a concentric circle of streets around the modest minaret of the Mulla Effendi mosque. Until 2007, when the Kurdistan Regional Government began restoring the citadel, 840 families lived within its confines. When evictions began so the renovations could take place, one family was allowed to remain, thus insuring that seven thousand years of settlement would continue uninterrupted.

Climbing the ramparts, Matt and I take in the sweeping vistas, the horizon replete with car dealerships, chain hotels, and the empty floor plans of uncompleted skyscrapers. Since the US invasion of Iraq in 2003, Erbil has been a boomtown, a beachhead of stability and progress, a promise of what a unified and peaceful Iraq could look like. With an uncompleted vision of the region's future laid before us, Matt and I begin to speculate. I tell him that being in Erbil makes me imagine what it must have been like to be in Barcelona in 1936. The Spanish Civil War, like the current conflict in Iraq and Syria, proved a prelude to a larger ideological crisis, between communism and fascism and democracy, one that defined Europe through the Second World War and through much of the twentieth century. Today the ideological tension in the Middle East is among the Islamists, as represented by groups like the Islamic State; the autocratic regimes, as represented by rulers like Bashar al-Assad in Syria and Abdel Fattah el-Sisi in Egypt; and the democratic activists, as represented by the now largely defunct movements that rose up during the Arab Spring.

Matt patiently listens to my theory, then asks how the Kurds fit into this construct. "I guess they don't. They're just our friends," I say, knowing that "friend of the United States" is a complex role to hold during an existential crisis in the Middle East. Slowly, we wander through the citadel's inner keep, passing beneath an enormous Kurdish flag. I remember the rusted cans of ammunition on the front near Makmour, the decade-old rifles the peshmerga used to hold the line against the Islamic State, and I wonder if we Americans are living up to our end of the bargain as friends.

Walking down the citadel's ramp toward the bustling souk Eskan, we again pass the sleepy guard in his chair. His attitude mirrors everyone else's: it seems impossible that the Islamic State, despite occupying positions only thirty minutes away from the city limits, could make any real incursion into the Kurdish stronghold of Erbil. Even if the United States provided less than adequate support for the peshmerga, it seems that they will hold the line regardless.

Having traveled extensively in the Middle East, I find it disorienting to be surrounded by Kurdish amity for the United States, instead of the animus I've grown accustomed to in other countries. I am again reminded of the Kurds saying "We have no friends but the mountains." After nearly a decade of investment, facilitated by the US occupation of Iraq, it seems like the Kurds can add "and the Americans" to this. In the war against the Islamic State, the Kurds have become an important ally, providing essential combat troops when a war-weary America will not send its own. But proxy war is a dangerous game, often turning friends into enemies: Afghanistan's mujahideen, Nicaragua's Contras.

A week after our walk through the citadel, I have returned to Istanbul and Matt has returned to Gaziantep. He sends me an email with a single article attached. The Islamic State has detonated a bomb, just by the citadel's portcullis, the first Erbil has seen in years, killing four and injuring twenty-two. The bomber was a local, his name Abdulrahman al-Kurdi.

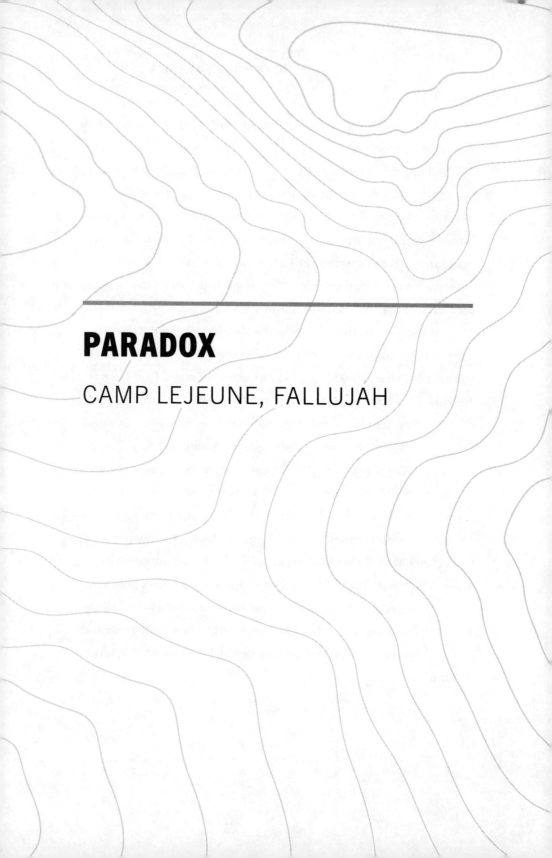

PARADOX

CAMP LEJEUNE, FALLUJAH

More than a year after the fall of Mosul, the Iraqi Army remains scuttled. American advisers return by the thousands to familiar camps like al-Taqaddum, an air base straddling the dark waters of Lake Habbaniyah. They disembark from helicopters, from transport planes, from Humvees, into a war that anticipates their return. Their old billets wait for them, huts of plywood construction. Office chairs lay toppled on the ground, strewn next to abandoned desks. Gloved hands right them, smacking four years of dust from seat cushions and armrests. This dust also coats desktops, where stacks of wilted magazines—*People, Us Weekly, Rolling Stone*—rest undisturbed, their covers dating from 2011. Everything is plywood: the desks, the walls, the floors. To build with cement or solid board would have suggested permanence in a war that began at its alleged end: *Mission Accomplished*. President Obama now heralds a different return: "If the Iraqis are not willing to fight for the security of their country, then we cannot do it for them." Conjuring an Iraqi will to fight—for Iraq—remains a decade-long waiting game. I recall another waiting game in these deserts, the one we played for the rain.

All through the summer of 2004, while our rifle platoon waged counterinsurgency in Haditha, Hit, and other Anbari backwaters that have since fallen to the Islamic State, it never rained, not once. Within the platoon we had a betting pool; ten bucks got you in: try your luck and pick the first day of rain. When the dust finally turned to mud on November 8, all forty-six of us were staged just outside of Fallujah, hunkered down in slit trenches, waiting for the assault to begin.

I don't remember anybody collecting on the pool.

All it takes is the sight of someone sprinting along a wet cross-walk and I'm back in Fallujah and back to that one street in particular: Highway 10. Veterans of the battle each have their story of crossing Highway 10's expansive four lanes covered by machine gun fire, with Islamists dug into the buildings on the far side, defending this, their main line of resistance. The story of Gunnery Sergeant Ryan Shane, a Marine from my infantry battalion, has always remained close. On the second day of the battle, his rifle platoon perched on a rooftop covering another platoon that rushed the crossing's gauntlet. Within minutes, a slug ripped through the leg of Sergeant Lonny Wells, a twenty-nine-year-old career Marine and father of four children, felling him in the open. He lay facedown, blood pooling around his waist, moving just a little. Leaving his rifle behind so it wouldn't slow him, Ryan went after Lonny.

A Marine combat cameraman captured the scene in four photographs. In the first, Ryan stands in the wet street, bent over Lonny. His 220-pound frame tugs the drag strap on Lonny's body armor. In the second, another Marine runs to Ryan's side, trying to help. Clumsily, the second Marine bends over Lonny while Ryan keeps pulling. The next frame is taken just as a bullet tears into Ryan's lower back, scrambling his stomach. He's on his heels, falling. The other Marine watches in a half sprint, heading for cover. The final frame is Ryan and Lonny, both lying facedown on the street in the rain.

Lonny is dead. Ryan will survive.

———

Nearly two years later, during the pivotal al-Anbar Awakening, when Sunni tribes united against al-Qaeda in Mesopotamia, fifty veterans of the Battle of Fallujah gathered in an auditorium in Camp Lejeune, North Carolina. Ryan Shane would be decorated for his actions. Since Lonny died, Ryan's 220 pounds had withered to 150. After countless surgeries, he'd been medically discharged from the Corps. The toll his stomach wound had taken on his body could be seen in his atrophied frame, but it was the forced separation from the Corps he loved that left the deeper wound. You could see that in his eyes.

I sat in my uniform a few rows back. We came to attention as the adjutant read the citation for Ryan's Bronze Star. Our commanding general pinned it on his chest and then ceded the floor to Ryan. He thanked all of us for coming to the ceremony. He thanked his family for their care during his slow, ongoing recovery. Then his voice thickened. He held his stare upward, into the glare of the auditorium lights, as if speaking to a place outside of this room.

"I'm finding it really hard," he said, "to accept that my greatest achievement as a Marine, this medal, also comes from my greatest failure. I didn't save Lonny that day."

Dangling from Ryan's shirt pocket was the scarlet ribbon pinned with a small brass V, which denotes valor—the conquest of fear. The fear Ryan must have felt as he ran onto Highway 10 is a sensation I am familiar with: that clench in the chest, that sluggishness of the limbs, the slowing of time, and the premonition of a violent death that lurks beyond each shut door you must shoulder open or alley you must sprint across. I know the way it makes my mouth dry. The way it has stalked me long afterward.

I can describe to you how fear feels, but not courage.

Courage is not an emotion. It's a virtue. You don't *feel* brave.

Then what did Ryan feel? What force overpowered his fear as he went after Lonny, compelling him to stand against the thick snaps of machine gun fire while he dragged his friend toward safety, until one of those snaps found its mark in his stomach?

Ryan and Lonny both served in Bravo Company, a close-knit group of nearly two hundred Marines. As a gunnery sergeant, Ryan mentored the younger noncommissioned officers, the corporals and the sergeants who, like Lonny, were coming up through the ranks. He and Lonny had trained for the better part of a year together and endured months of toil guarding an ammunition depot in the Iraqi desert before the battle. It's safe to say that Ryan saw a younger version of himself in Lonny. Ryan, as a senior enlisted Marine, was also a key leader in Bravo Company, and as such, he felt responsible for Lonny—he felt love for him.

Such love is the opposite of fear. It is why Ryan ran out to save Lonny.

Yet Ryan's feeling of failure reveals a painful paradox of combat. As he and Lonny lay bleeding in the center of Highway 10, our entire battalion, including our regiment and division, thousands of Marines, had phase lines our commanders had ordered us to reach. These phase lines, points of advance deeper inside Fallujah, indicated on the maps we carried, marked our mission for that day. We had to reach them, or fail. From the general commanding our division to the corporal commanding the three privates in his team, the mission came first. Before the Marines. This is the nature of war. If our lives took precedence, no hill would ever be taken, no building stormed or city seized, because some of us would die achieving this mission. The courage shown by Ryan, by Lonny, by many others, is essential to that success. It is a courage bred from love, from months spent training together, knowing each other's families, suffering shoulder to shoulder. Becoming friends. These bonds, fully realized, inspire incredible sacrifice in service of one another. And in service of the mission.

Therein lies the paradox.

The mission still comes first. The price is your friends. So you destroy what you love. This is the heartbreak I could hear in Ryan's voice. Your heart can't break if you weren't in love.

"A lot of people have asked me about that day," continued Ryan, "but nobody has ever asked who came to get me. After I was shot, there were two of us lying out along Highway Ten." His eyes fixed toward the back of the crowd, on two lance corporals, not much more than twenty years old, who would receive no recognition, except for this nod from Ryan, an acknowledgment of how they felt about each other.

One by one, we left our seats to shake Ryan's hand. Many of us would go on to more deployments in Iraq and Afghanistan, but a battle as big as Fallujah never came along again, though there were others like it.

In valleys, hamlets, and cities too countless to number, Ryan Shane's words held true. Our greatest achievements were tied to our greatest failures. It's a paradox as old as war: love is fear's opposite, the will to fight is ultimately bound with the will to destroy those you love, victory always couples with defeat.

Like a lot of guys, I learned this in the rain.

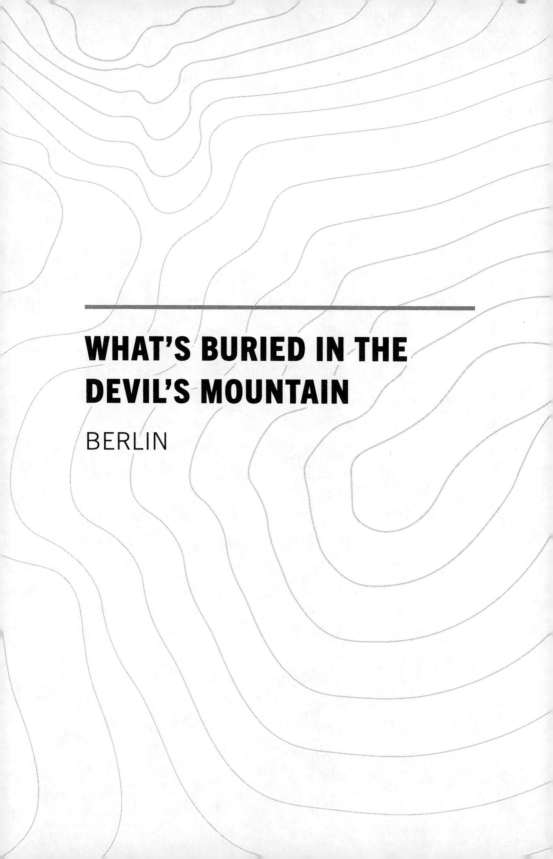

WHAT'S BURIED IN THE DEVIL'S MOUNTAIN

BERLIN

J ust before Christmas, I take my daughter Coco, who is now four years old, to Berlin for the weekend to visit Jack and his family who are now stationed there. This trip was nearly six months in the making, though its purpose is simple—Jack and I haven't seen each other in a year and we want to catch up. Maintaining our friendship has become important to me: when I chose to reenter civilian life after fighting in Afghanistan and Iraq, Jack and I had an argument about that decision which nearly ended that friendship. I had been slated to work as his deputy on a deployment to Afghanistan, but had pulled out at the last minute. As I wait for him on a bench in the arrivals terminal of Berlin's Tegel Airport, Coco curls up against me, clutching an iPad, her imagination transported by *The Princess Bride*, while my imagination becomes equally transported, staring out the window at an impenetrable lid of clouds.

Jack's a few years older than me, and though we're hardly old men, it now seems we were quite young when we first met. I was twenty-two, he was twenty-six, the two of us students at the Amphibious Reconnaissance School, the special operations course where one qualified to become an elite Recon Marine. That summer, not even a year had passed since the Twin Towers had collapsed. The Afghanistan War had

begun, the Iraq War hadn't, but we all wanted in on it. Jack was a lieutenant with a few years in the infantry and a couple of peacetime
deployments to Okinawa under his belt. I was still a Navy ROTC mid-
shipman, and this was my last summer in college before becoming an
officer. In Marine circles, the rigor of the course was legendary: hikes
with nearly one hundred pounds of equipment in the Virginia woods,
days without sleep on patrol, open ocean swims that went on for several miles. Less than a third of the Marines who started the Amphibious
Reconnaissance School graduated. There were many ways to wash out,
and succumbing to heatstroke was one.

A few weeks into our training, on a particularly hot July day, we
had a stalking exercise. Wearing heavy ghillie suits, a uniform covered
with burlap and used by snipers, our assignment was to crawl unseen
at a snail's pace for over a mile in order to sneak within a few yards of
an instructor who was searching for us with a set of binoculars. Having
not brought enough water, my canteens ran empty within a couple of
hours, and a couple of hours after that I was dangerously dehydrated.
Flat on my stomach, creeping toward the instructor, my vision began to
tunnel, and every time I flexed a muscle, pinpricks of light exploded
into view. In the early afternoon the instructor blew his whistle, the
signal that all of us should stand and show our progress. As I attempted
to come to my feet, I instead sunk to my knees. Almost immediately, I
felt a set of arms loop under mine. It was Jack. While a few instructors
shouted after him, asking if everything was all right, he dragged me
beneath a nearby tree, ripping off the bush hat I wore and dousing my
head in cold water from his canteens before a medic or anyone else
could realize I'd already suffered heatstroke. Then, once I'd gathered

myself, and with no one the wiser, we walked over to the trucks that would drive us to our barracks.

———

When Jack's minivan pulls up to the arrivals terminal, I am staring out at the overcast sky, the day holding just above freezing, thinking about the heat of that afternoon twelve years before and how my friend had saved me from washing out. Coco has fallen asleep watching her movie, and after I scoop her up in my arms, Jack helps me strap her into one of the three car seats in the minivan's back. With Coco securely napping, I gather our bags from the curb. "You look good," Jack says. I tell him he looks the same, which is to say neither good nor bad. He grins.

Driving in from the airport, we pass by the Tiergarten, a park in the heart of Berlin where Frederick the Great once hunted wild boar. An afternoon mist lurks between endless rows of linden trees, and through it I can see the distant Brandenburg Gate. I crane my neck to get a better look and catch a glimpse of Coco behind me, still asleep. I don't bother waking her. She won't remember the sights anyway. While I take in the view, Jack and I catch up—his work, my work, the evolving logistics of our lives. That evening, after dinner, we gather around the undecorated Christmas tree in his living room. His wife is out doing some holiday shopping, and his three girls absorb Coco into their pack. While Jack's daughters teach mine to dance to Taylor Swift and bedazzle her shoelaces, I feel how the context of our friendship has shifted onto a new foundation: the bond between two soldiers has become the bond between two fathers.

With our girls tucked into bed, the two of us sit in his living room, him drinking a whiskey and me a coffee. We pick up a bit of our conversation from the car ride, Jack telling me about his new job, which he doesn't love; me telling him about my move to Istanbul, which has been a challenge. We tell stories about old friends, some living, some dead, but we don't talk about the argument we had more than three years before, when I'd chosen to leave the service. Heading off to my bedroom, I wonder if we'll get to it that weekend.

⸻

After that summer at the Amphibious Reconnaissance School, I went back to college and Jack left for the invasion of Iraq. While he was embarked on a navy ship crossing the Atlantic toward Kuwait, the two of us swapped emails. His notes were filled with skepticism about whether the invasion would even occur; mine were filled with angst about missing the war. I even considered dropping out of college to enlist, leaving one semester shy of my degree. Then the invasion launched. I heard nothing from him for months, and I worried about my friend.

That summer, Jack returned home. Having seen some of the toughest fighting, he'd been decorated for valor, and I began my training as a new lieutenant. The next year, the two of us were back in Iraq but on opposite sides of the country. Now and again I'd bump into a captain or senior enlisted Marine who knew Jack. They always said he'd mentioned me, and often I found they'd sought me out just as a favor to him, to see how I was doing. When people asked about our friendship, I referred to him as my "Marine big brother." For years the two of us deployed in and out of Iraq, then later Afghanistan, never serving on the same battlefield but always finding one another when we returned home. Between these deployments, we'd keep up by going on long runs together.

The next morning, more than a decade after this all began, the two of us bundle up in the foyer of his home, heading out on another run while our daughters sleep.

Jogging out from his house, it is nearly seven a.m. but still dark. The two of us always get our miles in during the early hours; the quiet of that time seems to open a neutral space where we can offer up the guarded parts of ourselves—fears, frustrations, ambitions—and when we return in the day, these disclosures remain in that morning space. Weaving through narrow residential streets, we eventually find ourselves on the Kurfürstendamm, a broad avenue in the heart of Berlin. After a few miles we've spoken about the war in Syria, the pros and cons of sending our children to international schools, the Edward Snowden controversy, but still I feel us dancing around that old argument, which had also happened on a run, one looping a barren airfield in eastern Afghanistan, when I'd told him that deployment would be my last and I wouldn't be coming to work for him. It was the only run the two of us never finished.

There's a church where the Kurfürstendamm merges with the Kantstrasse. Burnt and jagged, its half-amputated spire reaches toward the night sky like a tree exploded by lightning. Steel bands reinforce the buckling pillars on the church's facade, and the cold winter air blows unrestrained through the stone-gabled windows and a gutted circular cavity once filled by a massive assemblage of stained glass. The Allies had bombed the Kaiser Wilhelm Memorial Church nearly seventy years before, leaving it partially in ruins. After the war it was never rebuilt. It stands as a reminder that remembrance and reconciliation are often one and the same.

Jogging in place on the sidewalk for a few moments, staring up at the spire, neither of us speaks. I want to say something but don't know quite how. "Pretty amazing," he says, "leaving it like that for everyone to see." And before I can answer he adds, "Let's get going." By now the morning's commuters have filled the sidewalks, and we turn back, dodging our way home through ever-thickening crowds.

We run the next two mornings, but I feel my chance to talk with Jack about our old argument evaporated in front of the Memorial Church. The days go by and we immerse ourselves in our children, taking them to the outdoor Christmas markets, walking with them in the expansive Grunewald Forest that abuts his house. The girls take to sleeping in the same room, making each night a slumber party. The older girls dress my daughter up like a princess, doting on her as if she were one of their younger sisters, and I think but don't say how this feels appropriate, Jack having always been a big brother to me.

The morning before I leave, we take a final run. Instead of heading through downtown Berlin as we've done the other days, we choose to take an easier route, through the Grunewald Forest. The floor of the forest is damp, silencing our steps. I think I might try one last time to bring up our disagreement, that old wound, how we hadn't spoken for a year afterward, how I wonder if he's now forgiven me. I begin by asking him if he remembers the stalking exercise from all those years ago, how he saved me from washing out, how hot it'd been that day. He doesn't say much, and I continue to recount everything I owe him: how he'd looked out for me during all those deployments, how he'd taken it upon himself to call up each new commander I worked for in the Marines and tell them I was a solid guy, how if he hadn't taken care of me that day in the sun my career and my life might have taken a different course. Still, Jack doesn't say much. I think he can tell where I'm going with all this talk. By now we've finished our run. Strolling through the forest, we come upon the banks of the lake, the Grunewaldsee. The sun is up, the day clear, and across the lake there is a hill. We are barely walking now.

"One of the things I love about running in this city," says Jack, "is that it's completely flat." Then he points across the lake, to the hill that overlooks the entire forest. "That's one of the highest points in Berlin. If you'd stayed longer, I would've taken you up there. It's got a great view."

I nod, trying to figure a way back into our conversation, but before I can say anything else, Jack goes on. "It's not real, though. The hill's man-made."

"Who made it?" I ask.

"After the Battle of Berlin, there was so much destruction lying around this city; rubble, tanks, artillery pieces, bodies—where do you put it all? You can't leave it out. So they buried it in a huge pile and covered it with dirt and grass. You know what they call it?"

I shake my head, no.

"The Teufelsberg—'Devil's Mountain.'"

Neither of us says much more. The particulars of that argument have become meaningless now. After three days together, Jack and I end our time in a quiet walk along the banks of the lake, looking at Berlin's only mountain, which looms as an ever-present yet camouflaged wound, integrated with—and thus inextricable from—the postwar topography of this city where we've met.

MY LAST MOVIE NIGHT

SHKIN

At Shkin firebase, a remote outpost in southeastern Afghanistan, Thursday night was movie night. There were three hundred Afghans in the special operations unit I advised during 2010 and 2011, and our handful of Americans would invite their leaders to our corner of the compound to relax. We'd hang a bedsheet between two guard towers to make a wide-screen, and begin the show. Picking something to watch was an exercise in hurdling cultural barriers. What film could you offer a group of grizzled Pashtun tribesmen, most of whom spoke no English? More times than I care to remember, we viewed *Rambo III* (the one where he fights the Soviets alongside the mujahideen) or *Troy* (which surprisingly, or perhaps unsurprisingly, needs no translation). As the opening credits rolled, we'd hand out popcorn and fill brown paper cups with Jim Beam for the Afghans who wished to join us. By the time Sly bagged his first communist or Brad diced up his first Trojan, the Afghans would be cheering, red-faced and all grins. In the back row of foldout chairs, two of the senior-most troopers always sat together, the platoon commanders Mortaza and Sabir. I'd take a place next to them, and beneath a flickering projector the three of us would quietly talk.

———

After a few years as an infantryman, I'd migrated over to special operations, and the men under my command were no longer Marines but foreign soldiers like Mortaza and Sabir. These two couldn't have been more different from each other, and yet, as is often the case, they were best friends. Mortaza was Pashtun, black-eyed with hawkish cheekbones and a wiry frame. Sabir was Tajik, eyes blue as new marbles, face like an anvil, built to absorb anything. The only physical similarity between them was their long hair and fierce, unkempt beards.

Good for a joke or prank on even the worst days—and worst days were plenty around Shkin—Mortaza was an easy guy to get along with. The first time we met, he was sprawled across the sofa in our operations center, watching Bollywood dance videos on the same flat-screen television where we'd sometimes pipe in the live feed from drone strikes. After our introduction he draped his arm around my shoulder, welcoming me to the unit but also taping a piece of paper to my back. It read *Khar*, "Donkey." Everyone laughed. Well versed in the dos and don'ts of locker room bravado by this point in my career, I took it with a smile, which made me okay in Mortaza's book. My first meeting with Sabir was more somber. He'd just returned from the machine gun range, the forty guys in his platoon shuffling behind him in a dusty column. Standing at the gate to our firebase, I offered my hand and my name. Sabir offered neither, and only fixed his eyes on mine. He asked me how many men I'd killed.

I was thirty-one years old then, and had collected as many dead friends as an eighty-one-year-old. My youthful desire to matter and make a difference had eroded, if it wasn't gone altogether. So why did I keep deploying? Was I drawn back to war because I couldn't find meaning outside it? I was tired and had begun to think about making this deployment my last. Having just had my first child, Coco, the pain of separation surprised me. Leaving on my first deployment since her birth, I stood in the departures terminal with Coco's small arms looped around my neck in a goodbye hug; it felt selfish to pry myself loose from her grip. I had been thinking a lot about bonds as a new officer in Shkin, both those with my family but also those I needed to form with the Afghans. Among the troops, these grew as we watched out for one another's lives on countless patrols. However, when it came to Mortaza and Sabir, I soon realized there was something they valued more than their lives: their hopes for their future—I guess you'd call these their dreams. And in the back glow of that Thursday night movie, this is what we usually discussed, their dreams as well as mine.

Mortaza would talk about Europe—Copenhagen, for some reason. "I will go there and rent an apartment," he'd say, "and not work for a while. I've saved money fighting; I'll spend it on girls and the disco." There were variations on this fantasy. Sometimes it'd be Stockholm, but always there were *girls* and a *disco*, and he would say this with his whole soul, his eyes piercing yours, making you believe that all the nobility of the free world resided in those two words.

Sabir's ambitions proved more conventional, not unlike mine. Both of us hoped to be good fathers despite the danger and long absences of our chosen profession. An ethnic Tajik, Sabir lived in the north of Afghanistan, in the Panjshir Valley, the epicenter of mujahideen resistance against the Soviets twenty-five years before. Living so far away, Sabir never used the ten days of leave the soldiers earned every two months. The trip would've taken him from our unit for weeks, the journey to the Panjshir being a long and difficult one. Despite the effect of his absence on his young son, just like me he'd set a pattern of putting his troopers ahead of his family.

I shared my own fears and hopes, offering up details of my daughter's earliest days: how she liked to sleep with the dog, the way she sometimes cried when she saw me on Skype with my own fierce beard, and, if we'd had enough to drink, my misgivings about a soldier's life, my concern that after fighting these many years I'd find a "normal life" boring, even trivial. I have plenty of war stories about Mortaza and Sabir—the ambush at Mangritay, a certain long patrol south of Gomal— but when they return to me now, whether I'm sitting up with my daughter in the middle of the night or riding a crowded bus along the seaside road in Istanbul, what I remember are those conversations.

———

We'd been out on patrol for three days, scouting a hilltop outpost near the Afghan-Pakistan border. It was cold, late November; frost crusted our field jackets and the barrels of our machine guns. The night before, we'd slept huddled in our trucks, nearly a hundred of us spread in a column. As the first light of the rising sun cast shadows across the peaks, the Afghan troops gathered in twos and threes around small propane stoves, heating tea, gnawing on bits of frozen bread. I gathered with Mortaza and Sabir, who were deep in discussion.

Sabir was planning to take leave when we returned from this patrol, his first since I'd known him. That night, a resupply helicopter was headed to our firebase. If Sabir got on it, he'd make it home days ahead of schedule. The two were debating the best route back, and Mortaza thought we should take a shortcut, one that ran across a plateau of hardpan desert, leaving us exposed to ambush by the Taliban but shaving hours off our return journey. "I've done it before," Mortaza explained. "Aside from a few washes, the ground is completely flat." When I looked at Sabir, I could see how much he wanted to be on that helicopter. I wanted to help him home, so I decided we should take the shortcut. Climbing into our trucks, I overheard Mortaza ask Sabir what he planned to do once he was with his son. Staring into his tea, then off to the mountains, then back into his tea, Sabir responded, "What did you do with *your* father as a boy?"

Mortaza said nothing.

We drove fast and hard, well into the afternoon. Here and there, our convoy of fifteen pickup trucks would dip into a wash, slowly crawling up the other side. Mortaza's platoon led the way, him up front acting as our guide. My truck traveled in the back of our column, with Sabir's platoon. We ate lunch on the move, never taking a break, all to get Sabir on his evening flight. By early evening, long shadows had spread from the ridgetops to the foothills. We'd make it, but only just. Dipping into a wash, our convoy bunched together. From its back, I strained up in my seat to see what the delay was; then my consciousness did a quick three-step: sight (*huge clods of earth spilling up, like a fountain*), thought (*Fuck, no*), sound (*a thunderclap*).

The IED tore apart the front vehicle in our convoy, blasting its doors from the hinges, incinerating its engine block. Then our Taliban ambushers began to shoot at us from a distant ridgeline, its slope popping and flashing, wild as paparazzi. We shot back from all our trucks, except for one. Immediately ahead of me, I saw Sabir peel off the column. Despite the danger of another IED, he'd gone to look for his friend.

———

That night, the helicopter that was supposed to take Sabir to his family took Mortaza to his. Before it landed at our base, the local mullah had readied his body for burial, as well as the three dead troopers who'd also been in the truck. In the center of the firebase's motor pool, we'd parked in a circle, our headlights shining in a ring, illumining the preparation of the dead while the mullah performed the ceremonial cleaning—sponges against skin and white linen wrapped around limbs, making the *kafan*, a burial shroud. As the mullah shaved Mortaza's beard and hair, cleansing him for the next life, Sabir cradled his best friend's head. Then he lowered Mortaza into his casket.

As the helicopter made a final approach to our firebase, we turned off our trucks' headlights so they wouldn't blind the pilot. Now it was pitch-dark and cold. As soon as the helicopter touched down, small clusters of soldiers rushed forward with the coffins, loading them. Then the helicopter's blades hacked at the dark sky, lifting the bodies away and pouring a surge of air from the engine over those of us who remained behind. That air, warm as breath, is my last memory of that night.

A few days later, it was Thursday again. Despite Mortaza's death, we hung up that sheet, filled our cups, picked a film. We weren't sure if the Afghans would show up, but they did, perhaps needing the escape this ritual provided. I found Sabir sitting on the foldout chairs in back. He was almost unrecognizable, having cut his beard and hair. I sat next to him. "You look young," I said, pointing to his clean-shaven face.

"I'll make my way home tomorrow," he said. Despite everything that had happened, I felt some solace—soon Sabir would see his son. But part of me wondered about his haircut. Had he got rid of his wild mane and beard so his child might recognize him, or was his haircut similar to Mortaza's, the return home signaling a certain type of death? Unlike wars past, Afghanistan wouldn't end but just seemed to drag on—no victory, no defeat—each of us having to declare a separate peace if we ever wished to return home. Mortaza's death felt singular to me even though I'd seen plenty of similar deaths before. It's just that I'd never seen them with the same eyes that looked at my daughter.

Sitting next to Sabir, I wondered how much longer he'd stay in the war and whether he blamed me or himself for Mortaza's death. I hoped even with Mortaza gone we might speak as we once had. But before I could say any of this, Sabir stood to refill his cup. When he came back he didn't sit with me but went over to sit with the rest of the Afghans. Without Mortaza our conversation seemed to be over. The next morning, Sabir was gone. A month later, that same helicopter returned, taking me home after what I'd now decided would be my last tour.

A week or so later, I sat in a barber's chair just off Connecticut Avenue in Washington, D.C. While my then-wife waited for me to trim my beard and tangled mop of hair into something manageable, Coco started to cry. She was nine months old now, and her mother took her and circled the block with the stroller while I sat in the barber's chair, watching a transformation take place—one I felt uneasy about—in the mirror.

I don't know if Sabir ever came back from leave. Perhaps he stayed in the Panjshir Valley with his son, deciding he'd had enough of the war. I often think of Mortaza too—how he'd do anything for a friend, his easy laugh, the disco and the girls. And that day getting my haircut became a memory I will always pair with those friends—the ritual of it, the letting go of one self for another. When the barber finished, he spun my chair around, then moved on to his next customer. Sitting alone, I waited for my daughter. I hoped she'd be satisfied with all that had been hidden beneath that beard and hair.

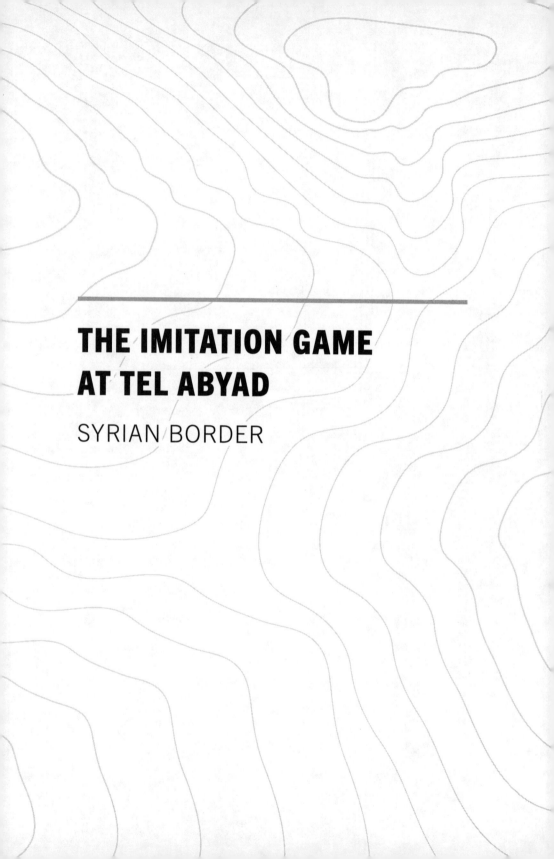

THE IMITATION GAME
AT TEL ABYAD

SYRIAN BORDER

gain the summer, and a fighting season: 2015. In the waning days of that winter, the Syrian Kurdish People's Protection Units, or YPG, dislodged the Islamic State from Kobane, denying them one of two key border crossings from northwestern Syria into Turkey. The other crossing, in the hardscrabble town of Tel Abyad, has just fallen to a coalition of YPG and Free Syrian Army (FSA) fighters. Tel Abyad is the name given to the Syrian side of the border. Akçakale is the name given to the Turkish side. This is where Abed and I had baklava with Abu Hassar a year and a half before, just as the Islamic State had begun to traffic fighters and equipment through this crossing to their capital thirty miles south in Ar-Raqqah. Despite their defeat in Kobane, recent victories over the Iraqi army in Ramadi and the Syrian army in Palmyra have lent the Islamic State an air of invincibility, or at least momentum, so news of its impending defeat sends a flock of media to the border crossing abutting the town.

Tuesday morning, I hitch a ride south with Matt, who after conducting a humanitarian needs assessment in Kobane plans to conduct a similar assessment in Tel Abyad, detailing the scope of the destruction and how much of the town will require rebuilding. The road is empty, not a car or truck on it, its centerline stabbing dead straight toward the horizon. Traffic, commercial and otherwise, has evaporated. One would be forgiven for thinking this evaporation was the work of the oppressive heat, but the real culprit is the fighting at the border. Matt has asked me to drive so he can make some calls. He scrolls through the contacts in his phone as I travel up the gearshift, holding us in fifth along the autobahn while the eastern sun holds in our faces. Matt's chatting away and has leaned back in his seat, his foot crossed onto his knee, as he speaks to friends, to loose acquaintances, to anyone with access to Tel Abyad. He hopes to be put in touch with displaced residents who have recently fled and who can give him a sense of the destruction's scope inside town. A few local fixers who are assisting journalists with their stories offer to help, if they can.

Time for lunch, but we stop only for gas. I top off our Peugeot and buy some cigarettes, a Coke, and a few chocolates, which quickly melt when I set them on the dash. We continue on the road that parallels the border for another thirty minutes. Guard towers picketing either side of no-man's-land appear with greater frequency. Coils of razor wire loop their pilings, layering in single, then double, then triple strands. Then the horizon gathers into forms: some low-slung buildings, a cluster of trees all shivering in the hot wind, finally Tel Abyad and Akçakale's outskirts. Entering the town, I anticipate the chaos of a battle's aftermath—refugees, wounded fighters, prisoners—but instead chaos manifests as news trucks, dozens of them, both regional and international, all painted white, with rooftop satellite dishes posturing skyward like a peacock's plumage.

Matt and I park the Peugeot on the shoulder, among the news vans. He swivels his head up and down the road, phone to ear, searching out a fixer he knows. I trail behind him and begin to mix among some of the correspondents, most of whom are packing up their things. News has been slow, they grumble. The day before, a handful of Islamic State fighters had crossed the border, surrendering to the Turkish authorities. Then, this morning, there had been some controversy as to whether the YPG, who, as Kurds, have long-standing grievances with Turkey, would be allowed to raise their flag over Tel Abyad. To the disappointment of the remaining correspondents, that controversy resolved itself anticlimactically when the YPG and FSA commanders decided that it would be best to avoid a provocation, and so chose to fly Free Syria's flag.

Little has happened, or so it seems, yet the story emerging across the media remains the defeat of the indomitable Islamic State. This is despite the particulars—likely fewer than a hundred Islamic State fighters killed, no reinforcements sent from Ar-Raqqah—suggesting that what we've witnessed is a strategic withdrawal in Tel Abyad, not a defeat. When the overarching narrative takes primacy over the actual events, the result is an imitation loop, in which the story informs the reality and vice versa. Telling a story about the apparent defeat of an adversary has real effects. It can increase support for the war abroad. It can help with recruitment. And it can affect the way soldiers conduct themselves on the battlefield, blurring the lines between combatant and actor—sometimes quite literally so.

Just across the border, I've been following the case of Michael Enright, an actor who held minor parts in *Pirates of the Caribbean: Dead Man's Chest* and *Knight and Day*. He is volunteering in the ranks of the YPG, and his situation reminds me of a saying we had in my platoon, during the Battle of Fallujah: "It's your favorite war movie and you're the star." The joke arose because we would find ourselves unintentionally, and often in the middle of combat, uttering ridiculous clichés, bags of cherries imported from an Oliver Stone or Francis Ford Coppola film script. One afternoon, pinned down by machine gun fire in a building, we'd used explosives to blow a breach into a wall so that we could escape. As the smoke cleared and we climbed into the street, I found myself screaming "Everybody on me! Move out! Move out!" I remember feeling quite aware, as I said this, that it sounded absurd, like some terrible John Wayne trope, but in that moment, I really did need everyone to gather around me, and we really did need to move out.

During that deployment to Iraq, many Marines I knew, guys in their late teens or early twenties, would behave as they thought Marines at war were supposed to behave: you smoke Marlboro Reds, you crisscross bandoliers of machine gun ammunition over your chest, you tuck an ace of spades into your helmet band. These are learned poses, adopted mainly from the Vietnam war films we'd all grown up watching: *Full Metal Jacket*, *Platoon*, *Apocalypse Now*. But our war was for real. Or was it? We were imitating a story. And when stories would be made from our war, first by the media and then by filmmakers, they would be stories rooted in the reality of our imitations.

Standing just outside of Tel Abyad, among the news vans, satellite dishes, and skittering journalists, the desire on display to fit the details into a Hollywood-worthy story is palpable. What do these events mean to the larger arc of the conflict? Are we watching a turning point? Could Tel Abyad be the Islamic State's Gettysburg or Stalingrad, the moment when the narrative of this long, grizzly war shifts toward some brighter future? Who knows, and I wonder at the consequences of seeking to play to a larger story.

It isn't long before Matt circles back to find me. As we begin to talk, a pack of kids swarm our legs, hawking bottled water like vendors at a rock concert. I ask if he's been able to get any information on the conditions inside Tel Abyad. What humanitarian aid do the residents need? How much of the town will require rebuilding?

Matt shakes his head.

"All of the fixers I know have left," he says. "The story's gone elsewhere."

Our stomachs tell us it is well into the afternoon. Walking back to the Peugeot, Matt suggests we stop for a snack on the return to Gaziantep. I open the driver's door and the baking car heaves out a hot breath. I push and pull the door in an attempt to fan out the heat. Then we drive west with the windows down. As we rushed to Tel Abyad there was a stop I hadn't had time to make, but with the day's events resolved, I tell Matt that I want to find Abu Ali's shop, which is on this road. I am hoping he can tell me what's become of his brother, Abu Hassar.

We drive for less than fifteen minutes and then slow to a crawl. A year and a half ago, when Abed and I had made this trip, the land was rain-sodden. Now shimmers of heat desiccate the earth. Ahead of us dust stains the distant pavilions of Akçakale refugee camp, while an occasional cyclonic breeze scatters dirt skyward in tossed handfuls. We drive closer, coming to the road's shoulder where I'd dropped Abu Hassar off before and to the ditch where I'd watched the old couple draw water. The camp's residents shelter themselves inside their tents, avoiding the midday sun. The road is empty, an unwelcome premonition.

We park in front of Abu Ali's shop, which has no sign or adornment, just bare cement walls. There are a few half-empty inventory racks placed out front: potato chips, packaged cookies, dented boxes of candy bars whose brands I've never heard of. The shop's door is shut. No one lingers outside. Then I tug the door handle and the room opens into a crowded cross-section of mustachioed, stubbled, paunchy or underfed Syrians. Cigarette smoke wafts up toward dueling air-conditioning units, which these men gather beneath like the chieftains of some lost tribal council. Their voices hum with a kind of throaty warble. Mixing with that noise, as well as with the stench of midday sweat, is the gentle tinkling of teacups on saucers.

"Abu Ali?" I ask.

My request is met with quiet consideration, as if I have just put a motion before this tribal council for review. Somebody lights a cigarette. Somebody else stubs one out. Matt gathers some bottled waters, some cakes, a few more chocolates. He sets them by a cash register on a chest-high counter. From behind the counter Abu Ali stands. His manicured hands sort through the few items Matt has picked. He plucks the cigarette from his lips so that he can mouth out some basic arithmetic. Nicotine stains line his teeth like tidal markers. When Matt brings over two extra bottles of water, Abu Ali runs his fingers through his thinning hair as he does the last of the math.

"Do you remember me?" I ask before he announces how much we owe.

I've interrupted his calculation, and he flicks his eyes up.

"Abu Hassar," I say, pressing the two edges of my index fingers together in a gesture that among Arabs means "friendship." Something clicks, like Abu Ali has just found the equal sign he's been searching for, and he begins to nod in rapid fire. He then ducks beneath the counter.

Before I can explain that I am hoping to see his brother again, to reprise our conversation, to hear what's become of him in this eventful year; before I can say any of that, he has shooed away two of the men who'd been sipping tea in his shop and he has installed both Matt and me in the center of the day's gathering.

At first Abu Ali speaks quickly, and in Arabic. Then I speak slowly, and in English. Then he speaks slowly and in Arabic. Then neither of us says anything. We can't understand one another. Silently, we sip our tea.

"Why don't you call Abed?" Matt says.

Thankfully, Abed picks up. I tell him that I'm with Abu Ali, that I'm hoping to track down Abu Hassar—will he explain this to Abu Ali? And would he be interested in sitting down with Abu Hassar again? I haven't run any of this by Abed.

"Okay," he says. "Pass the phone to Abu Ali."

When Abu Ali hears Abed on the other end of the line, a smile tugs toward his ears and he reprises his rapid-fire nods. He says something to Abed, laughs, says something else, and then laughs again. Then his expression attunes toward listening. He leans forward, elbows on knees, pulls a cigarette from his shirt's front pocket, lights it, and keeps listening. He exhales toward the ceiling, then answers Abed and hands me the phone.

"He says no problem."

"So Abu Hassar is around to meet?" I ask Abed.

"Not exactly." Abed then explains that Abu Hassar had to leave his family in Akçakale to earn a living at a labor camp in Sakarya, an industrial city two hours outside of Istanbul. "Let's discuss it when you get back," he adds, and then hangs up.

I pocket my phone. Matt comes to the counter where he's left the snacks and water he'd gathered up. He takes money from his pocket to pay, offering it to Abu Ali, who refuses and who has now taken out his own cell phone, distractedly dialing a number. Matt insists, pulling a few bills from his wallet and leaving them out. Abu Ali also insists, stuffing them back into Matt's pocket. Then, as he's pushing us out of his store with our free snacks and water, he stops me at the door and holds up the phone. He points to the receiver. "Abu Hassar," he says, and hands it to me, so I might speak with him.

But I wave the phone away, not wanting to stumble along in half languages. "Please tell him that I'm coming," I say. Vacantly, Abu Ali stares back, piecing together whatever I've told him.

Then he resumes his nods.

———

Abed would've made the trip down to Tel Abyad that day, but he's quit working with Matt. An opportunity has come his way, one he needs to take, at the expense of his job—though Matt is understanding—and possibly at the expense of his relationship with his Swiss fiancée, Laetitia.

Soon after Abed first fled Syria for Beirut, he found his way from there to Egypt, where he and Laetitia had lived for nearly a year and where she had finally accepted his marriage proposal. Running short on money, Abed needed work; this is when Matt offered him a position at SREO in Gaziantep. Following a long separation from Abed, Laetitia has found a job at CARE International, a humanitarian aid organization with an office in Gaziantep. After having been forced apart for nearly a year while Laetitia remained in Egypt, this new job will allow them to again live with one another. At least that was the plan, until on a whim Abed applied for a scholarship to a prestigious master's degree program at University of Saint Andrews in Scotland. He never thought he'd get in.

Returning from Tel Abyad, I make dinner plans with Abed for the next night. He picks a Syrian restaurant in the posh Ibrahimli neighborhood near Matt's offices. The restaurant is vast, built to accommodate the elaborate spring weddings of the local industrialists who own the textile factories that skirt the city. The night is hot, so we sit inside in the air-conditioning and sip soda while a teenage busboy in a kitsch sequined vest and skullcap lights paper lanterns outside in the garden. Abed stares at the base of his Coke bottle, turning it on the table between his index finger and thumb. A little ring of condensation eats away at the paper tablecloth. "You know I'd like to see Abu Hassar too," Abed says. "It's just, things are quite difficult right now."

A few weeks before, I'd foolishly asked Laetitia where she and Abed planned to honeymoon after their wedding, scheduled at the end of the summer in Switzerland. Laetitia, who is gentle and courteous, and who usually speaks just above a whisper, snapped, "There isn't going to be a honeymoon, because Abed has chosen to leave me here so he can go to Scotland."

Abed continues to twirl his Coke bottle, his eyes averted from mine. "I talked with Abu Hassar a bit today," he says. "Abu Ali gave me his number."

"And?" I ask.

He glances up. "He wants to see us."

"And you?"

"I want to see him," says Abed.

"So come to Istanbul."

Abed looks back at me. "The wedding's going to be beautiful."

He talks about Lake Neuchâtel, an abbey on its banks, the Alps, but he stumbles over the descriptions, conjuring places he's heard of but never seen. Then he becomes quiet. A long passage of silence hovers between us. To break it up, Abed flags down our waiter, ordering for both of us. He and the waiter then enter an extended conversation in Arabic, one that seems to range beyond our order, and one in which Abed seems far more at ease than when he is recounting the particulars of his master's program in Scotland or his wedding in Switzerland.

The waiter heads to the kitchen and Abed goes back to fiddling with his Coke bottle on the paper tablecloth. Then he looks up at me.

"How far did you say it was to Abu Hassar's place in Sakarya?"

"A two-hour drive," I say.

Abed cups his chin with his hand. "Two hours. He's so close."

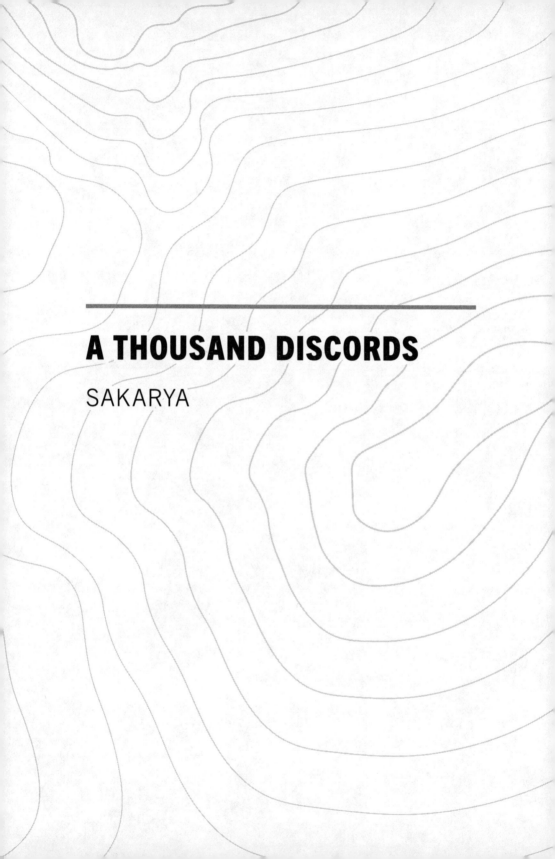

A THOUSAND DISCORDS

SAKARYA

The night before we drive to Sakarya, Abed sits on my living room sofa in Istanbul as I prepare my children for bed. I drape my daughter's nightgown over her raised arms. I fasten my son's diaper while he fusses at me. Then I shuttle them toward their bunk. They demand that our guest read them a story. Abed edges his way onto the bottom bunk. My children fall all over him and tug a book onto his lap, a compendium of fairy tales from around the world. My son's favorite is "Baba Yaga," a Slavic variant on "Hansel and Gretel," where a witch waits for children who wander too far into dark woods.

The next morning, Abed and I take to the road early, heading east. Our route to Sakarya skirts the Sea of Marmara, a shimmering table set with anchored freighters. We speed past them, winding nimbly up switchbacks, then across the mountain roads that abut the industrialized coast. Cranes dip over the harbors and smokestacks jut upward. But the operator cabins are empty and the furnaces aren't lit; it is Sunday.

Abed holds his phone to the passenger window. He snaps a picture of the vista below us. As he does, WhatsApp chirps with a new message. Abed begins to peck at his phone, composing a response. Then he glances up at me. "Abu Hassar's anxious for his baklava. He's asking when we'll be there."

In a box on the seat behind us are the two dozen pieces Abed brought from Gaziantep. I hadn't asked him to do this, and the fact that he brought them reminds me that Abed's connection to Abu Hassar is as real as my own.

I check my watch. "We should get in by eleven o'clock," I say.

Abed nods and resumes pecking out a response on his phone. When he finishes neither of us speak, as if saving ourselves for our lunch and the discussion to come. Then we turn inland. The Sea of Marmara disappears and the hills rise up behind us. The countryside becomes lush, overgrown with a canopy of shaded trees that we pass beneath, heading deeper into dark woods.

———

We park just opposite the Meydan, which is the main square in Sakarya. The streets are lined with retail outlets I've never heard of: clothing and electronics stores, cheap boutiques. All are shuttered. Teenage boys sweep the sidewalks in front of a few cafés while tweedy old men with pageboy hats wander inside, their wizened fingers clutching folded newspapers and backgammon boards. The police are out in force too, caps pulled low, one hand resting on the grip of their submachine guns and the other holding Styrofoam cups of morning coffee. Before I can ask Abed what he makes of the police, the two of us notice a band of migrant workers, apparently Arabs, assembling a steel reviewing stand in front of an Atatürk statue. It seems there will be a parade. I park our rental car along the main road leading into the Meydan.

While I pay the meter and struggle to read the parking notifications, Abed remains in the front seat, texting with Abu Hassar. I wonder why he doesn't just phone him, but then I remember how after a long separation from my family I never want to sully the moment of reunion by calling just beforehand.

Then Abed springs from his seat. *"Merhaba!"*

I'm bent over, feeding change into the meter, but straighten up at the sound of his voice. Abed slams the car door shut. A man in a neatly pressed short-sleeve shirt with khakis and Nike trainers wanders toward us. His hair is carefully combed, split neatly in a part. An ear-to-ear grin spreads across his face: it is Abu Hassar.

"Merhaba!" he calls back to Abed, laughing as he speaks a Turkish hello to his Syrian friend. Gone are his *as-salaam alaikum*'s from our last meeting. When the two of them embrace, I am within arm's length, and Abu Hassar clutches after me with the same affection a drowning man might show to a limb of passing driftwood. As we exchange our hellos, I wonder whether Abu Hassar's secular greeting and reformed appearance indicate a change of heart or a change in circumstances as he ekes out a wage working among the Turks.

I tell Abu Hassar that he looks good. His cheeks flush and he self-consciously hangs his head toward his shoes.

"Shukran," he says.

The three of us amble slowly through the Meydan, past the Turkish police with their coffees and submachine guns, past the closed stores, and past the Atatürk statue with the grandstand assembled in front.

"What's going on here?" Abed asks Abu Hassar, pointing to the gathering.

"A parade," he answers, "for soldiers leaving to fight the Kurds."

Just a month before, the pro-Kurdish Peoples' Democratic Party, or HDP, won an unprecedented 13.1 percent of the vote in national elections. This victory made it impossible for President Recep Tayyip Erdoğan to form a government, so he devised a strategy to undermine the HDP. After scheduling a snap reelection for November, five months after the original election, President Erdoğan then breaks a two-year-old ceasefire with Kurdish separatists in both southeastern Turkey and across the border in northern Iraq, bombing positions in the Qandil Mountains where Matt and I had driven with Dara just a few months before and where the Kurds are fighting the Islamic State. Erdoğan imagines everyday Turks will be less sympathetic to a pro-Kurdish party if Kurdish separatists are combatting the Turkish state.

"I should march in the parade," Abu Hassar says.

"Why would you do that?" I ask.

"It'd be the easiest way for me to go back to Iraq to fight the Kurds."

Neither Abed nor I say anything. It takes a moment for us to parse Abu Hassar's suggestion, in which the Kurds are a common adversary to both the Turks and the Islamic State. In the past three years, a two-sided war—rebels versus the regime—has become so multidimensional that a measure of logic exists in Abu Hassar's proposal. Before either of us can reply, he leans toward me. "What's that?"

Beneath my arm, I'd been carrying the box of baklava.

He forgets about fighting and we install ourselves at a sidewalk café along the Meydan.

The stray cats have two speeds: they either shuttle under the café tables, scrambling after food scraps, or they slowly wend through the shade cast by the Meydan's heavy-limbed elms. Suited old men fill the tables around ours. They nose at their newspapers and smoke with abandon, the clouds of tobacco lifting behind the pages. When a cat comes too near them, they kick it. The resultant hiss mixes with the rhythmic clacking of backgammon counters. Rising just above the backgammon, the voices of the old Turks can be heard arguing. It is an absentminded type of arguing, one that hardly ever causes them to look up from their game or their papers, but with an election coming up I can't help but imagine the subject is politics.

Our waitress sets down three cups of tea. Steam tumbles off the top of the curving, oblong glasses. I set out the baklava, offering it to Abu Hassar, who takes the box from me and insists that Abed have the first piece, which he does. Then an awkwardness arises. None of us knows how to pick up where we left off nearly two years ago.

I take a piece of baklava.

"You look different," I say to Abu Hassar, and then fill my mouth.

Abu Hassar has also just had a piece, and for a moment we chew silently. Then he swallows and drinks some tea. "Much has happened since I saw you last. This time has passed like prison time. When Assad arrested me, I learned in three years what most learn in a hundred and fifty."

"So what have you learned?" I ask.

Abu Hassar turns to Abed, speaking as if I've left the room. "He thinks asking questions is the same as listening." Then Abu Hassar turns back toward me. "It's not what I have learned but what you have."

His phone begins to ring. Before he answers it, he leans across the table and clasps my arm in sympathy, as if consoling a vanquished adversary. I light a cigarette in front of him, which I've never done before, not wanting to offend this pious Muslim. He shakes his head at me. Leaning back in his seat, he takes his call while I sit across from him saying nothing, just smoking.

Abu Hassar plants his elbows on the table, clutching his phone to his ear. With his chin hung toward his chest, he listens nervously to whatever he's being told. Then he flings his head back. An enormous smile pinches at his temples. I think I can see tears beginning to form. Then he turns away. Overcome by this rush of joy, he covers his eyes with his free hand. He gathers himself enough to speak between small bursts of laughter that threaten to descend into sobs.

Abed whispers, "His brother and sister have just arrived safely in Greece."

Abu Hassar quickly finishes his call. He sets his phone on the table between us and then pulls a piece of paper from his pocket. "Excuse me," he says. "I have one more call to make." And he begins to dial. While he waits for the call to connect, his countenance sets. I recognize this look, the resolve and the skepticism. I remember it from our first meeting in Akçakale. Someone answers the phone, but Abu Hassar doesn't offer a *salaam alaikum* or even a *merhaba*. He speaks to whomever is on the other end crisply. Though I don't understand what's being said, it is clear orders are being given. Abu Hassar's warmth from a moment before is gone.

Once again, Abed explains in a whisper: "That's the smuggler. He has to arrange for the other half of his siblings' payment."

The two of us remain respectfully quiet while Abu Hassar negotiates this last part of a deal, which I can only imagine has been some time in the making. He holds out his hand, searching for a pen. I pass him the one I keep in my notebook, and he takes it without a smile or a thank-you. He scribbles out a couple of notes on his pad. Then he gives a couple more orders. The call is over and he hands me back my pen. If Abu Hassar is curt with the smuggler, it's to be understood. Just two days ago the image of Aylan Kurdi, a drowned three-year-old Syrian whose family was betrayed by their smuggler, appeared on the front page and home page of countless news organizations.

In the photo Aylan rests cheek down in the sand, as if napping on his stomach. His shoes are still on, and he wears blue shorts and a red T-shirt. His family had left for Greece from Bodrum in Turkey, a peninsula crowded with resorts that cater to wealthy internationals. A suite with a seafront view goes for around a thousand euros a night. And each night, beneath the wrought iron balustrades of luxury hotel balconies, or just a bit further down the beach, smugglers land their rubber rafts in the soft sand. After paying the same price per head as a night's stay in Bodrum, Aylan Kurdi and his father, mother, and five-year-old brother left a nearby beach at three a.m. As they rode the channel between Turkey and Greece, so too did the Meltemi winds, which heaved up overhead swells. When Kurdi's raft threatened to capsize, their smuggler leaped overboard. Aylan's father tried to pilot the raft. Then it flipped. By the next morning the entire family, except for the father, had drowned.

Now finished with the smuggler, Abu Hassar pulls up a picture of Aylan on his phone. "This is all Assad's doing," he tells me.

"The boy's last name was Kurdi," Abed says to Abu Hassar, as if scolding him. "He was from Kobane."

Assad's forces haven't been in Kobane in years. The fight there is between the Islamic State and the Kurdish YPG, not the regime. Still, Abu Hassar isn't altogether wrong: the war would've been finished long ago if Assad had stepped down. But Abed isn't wrong either: the Islamic State has hijacked the war for its own purposes. Then again, with its dreams of an independent Kurdistan, so has the YPG.

Nobody says anything.

Our waitress, a teenage Turkish girl, refreshes our glasses of tea. "*Çok shukran*," says Abu Hassar, blending the Turkish word for "much" with the Arabic for "thank you." The waitress nods her head, giving Abu Hassar a sympathetic grin. She heads back toward the kitchen.

I ask Abu Hassar if he'll join his brother and sister in Europe. He gingerly sips from his hot glass. "I don't think so," he says, and then pulls out his phone to show me a posting on Facebook. It is a photograph of the German chancellor Angela Merkel. Beneath it is a quote in Arabic: *We will tell our children that Syrian migrants fled their country to come to Europe although Mecca and Muslim lands were closer to them.*

Since the beginning of the war, wealthy Arab nations such as Saudi Arabia and the Emirates have taken zero Syrian refugees, yet the German government has suspended the 1990 Dublin Regulation, which once mandated that refugees seek asylum in the first European country they enter, thus making settlement in countries like Germany, France, or Britain virtually impossible for those heading overland from Syria. With the suspension of the regulation, Angela Merkel has effectively opened up much of Europe to Syria's refugees, making her a hero among them. Abu Hassar shows me another photograph: it's a shot of Merkel superimposed on a heart-shaped Syrian flag.

"Will you go to Europe?" Abu Hassar asks Abed.

"No," he says, staring into his tea. His curt answer hides his uncertainty. Abed wants to remain engaged in Syria and what's left of his revolution. He also wants to start a life, to marry Laetitia, to have children. None of this can happen in his current limbo.

"Merkel is a start," says Abu Hassar, "but ultimately justice only comes through Islam." Then Abu Hassar reaches for my pen. He lays a napkin flat on the table. Like at our last meeting, he begins to draw a map. First, the long northeast-to-southwestern diagonal of the Syrian-Iraqi border, and then extending south to the desert kingdom of Jordan, and west to the Mediterranean coast. He fills in the names in Arabic. As he scrawls out Lebanon, I nod and point just to the south. "Yes, and Israel."

Abu Hassar fixes his eyes with mine.

"Palestine," he sternly replies, and inks the name onto his map.

Abed laughs. "Must you always remind him that you're half-Jewish?"

Abu Hassar takes his pen and places a heavy dot on the part of the map that is northeastern Syria, not far from the Islamic State's capital in Ar-Raqqah. He circles the dot and writes a name next to it. "Justice will come in Dabiq."

"Where?" I ask.

"In Dabiq the armies of the West will fight the Islamic armies of the East in a great end-of-days battle. Our armies will be led by the Mahdi. And God will make his judgment."

I lean back in my booth. Outside, the cats continue to chase one another, fighting after scraps of food from our café. Some street kids have begun to play tag in an emptied public pool, trapping each other in its corners. When Abu Hassar had delivered his polemics before, about the end of days, about the Mahdi, about judgment, they'd been easier to hear. Perhaps this was because we were in Akçakale, just a few hundred yards from the war, and his appearance conformed to my expectations of a jihadist: his thick beard, his olive-green keffiyeh, his field jacket. Now we are in a modern Turkish city, a European city. His beard is trim. His hair well combed. Dressed as he is, I wouldn't give him a second look on the street.

"So Abu Bakr al-Baghdadi is the Mahdi?" Abed asks.

"No," he says. "I told you last time: the Mahdi has yet to come."

"When does he come?" I ask.

"This is uncertain. There is a missing link in this chain of events, one I'm confused about." Abu Hassar reaches into his pocket. He sets his phone between us on the table and opens up an app; it is some sort of e-Qur'an. After tapping out a quick search, Abu Hassar pulls up a verse from the Kitab al-Fitan, a holy text similar to the Christian Book of Revelations:

وَإِنَّ أَهْلَ بَيْتِي سَيَلْقَوْنَ بَعْدِي بَلاَءً وَتَشْرِيدًا وَتَطْرِيدًا حَتَّى يَأْتِيَ قَوْمٌ مِنْ قِبَلِ الْمَشْرِقِ مَعَهُمْ رَايَاتٌ سُودٌ فَيَسْأَلُونَ الْخَيْرَ فَلاَ يُعْطَوْنَهُ فَيُقَاتِلُونَ فَيُنْصَرُونَ فَيُعْطَوْنَ مَا سَأَلُوا فَلاَ يَقْبَلُونَهُ حَتَّى يَدْفَعُوهَا إِلَى رَجُلٍ مِنْ أَهْلِ بَيْتِي

The people of my Household will face calamity, expulsion and exile after I am gone, until some people will come from the east carrying black banners. They will ask for something good but will not be given it. Then they will fight and will be victorious, then they will be given what they wanted, but they will not accept it and will give leadership to a man from my family.

"The men with the black banners are the Islamic State?" I ask. "And the 'man from my family' is the Mahdi?"

"I'm not sure," says Abu Hassar. Then he digs around in his phone some more, entering another search. "There is also this text from the Kitab al-Fitan."

إذا رأيتم الرايات السود فالزموا الأرض ولا تحركوا أيديكم ولا أرجلكم! ثم يظهر قوم ضعفاء لا يوبه لهم، قلوبهم كزبر الحديد، هم أصحاب الدولة، لا يفون بعهد ولا ميثاق، يدعون إلى الحق وليسوا من أهله، أسماؤهم الكنى ونسبتهم القرى، وشعورهم مرخاة كشعور النساء حتى يختلفوا فيما بينهم ثم يؤتي الله الحق من يشاء

When you see the black banners, remain where you are and do not move your hands or your feet. Thereafter there shall appear a feeble folk to whom no concern is given. Their hearts will be like fragments of iron. They are the representatives of the State. They will fulfill neither covenant nor agreement. They will invite to the Truth, though they are not from its people. Their names will be honorifics whose ascriptions will be to villages, or places. Their hair will be long like that of women. They shall remain so till they differ among themselves, and then God will bring forth the Truth from whomever He wills.

"The second one sounds more like the Islamic State," says Abed.

Abu Hassar slides his phone back into his pocket. He looks out the café's window. His westernized appearance seems a contradiction to his dogma. Contradiction is hardwired into the religious texts he quotes. It is hardwired into war too: feeling fear to express courage, forfeiting freedoms to protect them, and, of course, killing for peace.

And I think Abed senses this too, when he asks, "What will you do?"

"I am waiting," he says. "This battle will come. The Islamic State is one link in the chain that will take us closer to the final judgment."

"So you would fight in the final judgment?" I ask.

"If it happens in my lifetime, of course."

"Let's have some food," interrupts Abed. He waves down our waiter. Among the three of us, Abed speaks the best Turkish. He orders an eclectic mix: chicken schnitzel, a plate of kebab, two bowls of spaghetti. Abu Hassar asks for a Sprite. The two of us order Pepsi.

"After the final judgment you won't be able to find a Sprite," I say.

Abu Hassar laughs. "You are worried about Dabiq. Don't worry. If I see you there, I'll turn the other way."

I fish my phone from my pocket. I do a quick Google search and find a photograph of myself online. It's from my time in the Marines. I am in Afghanistan, with a thick beard. I am wearing a camouflage field jacket, not dissimilar in style to the one Abu Hassar wore at our last meeting. About twelve of us are in the photo, with rifles slung across our chests, our body armor laden with magazine and grenade pouches. Our helmets and radio microphones hide our faces.

Abu Hassar tucks his chin as he ponders the photo, seemingly uncertain of what he's looking at. "This is the army that will meet us?" he asks. I take the phone back and reverse-pinch my fingers across the screen so it zooms in on my face. He leans closer and points. "Oh, yes, I didn't recognize you."

"Would you recognize me at Dabiq?" I ask. "Would I recognize you?"

Abu Hassar then explains with great precision how one-third of the Christian armies of the West will convert to Islam before the battle and this is how the Eastern armies will triumph, so I shouldn't worry about whether or not he can recognize me at Dabiq, because all I need to do is convert to Islam and I will be spared.

"Like Peter Kassig," I say, referring to the aid worker and former US Army Ranger whom the Islamic State kidnapped and later beheaded, even after he converted and changed his name to Abdul-Rahman.

"You say Peter Kassig," he answers. "I say Abu Ghraib. An eye for an eye."

Abed has begun to knead his hands together, becoming impatient with our circular arguments. "If you practice an eye for an eye," he asks us, "do you know what you end up with?"

Abu Hassar and I stop our debate.

"You end up with a bunch of cut-out eyes."

A muezzin breaks into the first notes of the afternoon call to prayer, scuttling the pigeons that have flocked around a nearby minaret. The sound of flapping wings mingles with the wailing call, and the birds land around our café, mingling with the stray cats. Abu Hassar glances at his watch, leans toward me, and clasps my bicep. "Excuse me for a moment," he says, and then looks at Abed, as if questioning whether he'll join him in the mosque. Abed stays in his seat.

The muezzin's notes seem to stir some conciliatory impulse in Abu Hassar. They stir an opposite impulse in me. The call to prayer reminds me of foot patrols so numerous they blend into a loop. Dusty paths in Iraq or Afghanistan. High cement and mud walls. The perceived threat lurking behind each one. And our interpreter walking alongside me, his steady, whispered translation: "They are announcing our movements. They are calling to the fighters. They are predicting our death." The wail that calls out to God becomes indistinguishable from the wail that calls out for violence. Both are in a language I can't understand.

A Turkish friend of mine, a columnist whose journalist father was assassinated by a car bomb when he was a teenager, recounted to me a recent trip to Serbia for the twenty-year commemoration of the Srebrenica Massacre, a genocide of eight thousand Bosniak Muslims at the hands of Christian paramilitaries. Despite the passage of time, the war's tensions still simmered in this community. The authorities continued to exhume bodies from newly discovered mass graves—136 fresh corpses during my friend's visit—while international war crimes tribunals created equal measures of reconciliation and resentment. When not covering the commemoration, he found himself lingering in any neighborhood with a mosque nearby. Although he's not a particularly devout Muslim, upon returning to Istanbul he described the relief of driving home from the airport toward a horizon of minarets. When I told him how the sight of a minaret or the sound of a muezzin elicits in me a different response entirely, he shrugged. "I guess we would call this phenomena 'the relativity of minarets.'"

After just a few minutes, Abu Hassar slides back into the booth next to Abed. He begins to fiddle with his fork, refreshed by a new energy. I notice some markings on his forearm. Bundled against the cold at our last meeting, I hadn't seen what seems to be a tattoo. When I ask him what it is, he turns his forearm toward me. The script is shamrock green, cut without curves, straight as the razor that likely incised these marks. There are three letters: *N O R.*

Light.

Abu Hassar lifts a sleeve, where the letters appear again on his bicep in Arabic: نور.

"She is my beloved, though not my wife."

They met when he was seventeen and she was a bit younger. Her parents didn't approve of him. When I ask why, he smiles. "Maybe it was because I got her name tattooed on my arm?" Her parents' position forced them to meet secretly. If Abu Hassar wanted to speak to or see her, Nor's best friend would call her and hand Abu Hassar the phone. Eventually Nor's parents found their daughter a more suitable match. They had no future as a couple, so Abu Hassar told her to marry. Her new husband then moved them to Saudi Arabia, where Nor still lives.

"It must have been difficult when her whole family rejected you," I say.

"Not her whole family," Abu Hassar tells me. "Her brother and I fought alongside one another in Iraq. He was a great commander, but Assad's regime arrested him at the same time they arrested me, and when I was released he wasn't. No one has heard from him in eight years. I like to think that he's alive." Abu Hassar glances down, considering his arm and Nor's name inked into it. "Fighting in Iraq was difficult. Prison was difficult. Nothing was as difficult as losing Nor. She is still my beloved."

I ask if he's spoken with her since.

"No," he says, "it wouldn't be appropriate. My wife wouldn't approve. She knows about Nor and me."

"You told her?" I ask.

"I didn't have to. My wife was the one who used to call her on my behalf. She was Nor's best friend."

Abu Hassar asks me if a Western woman would understand such a thing. Before I can answer, Abed does. "Western women are different," he says. Then he points at me. "Last night, I saw him change his son's diaper." Abu Hassar begins laughing. Abed adds, "It was a disaster." And I'm uncertain whether he is referring to my diaper-changing skills or to the Western societal conventions that have made me a diaper changer.

"I don't imagine I'll see either of you in Europe then."

Abu Hassar stops laughing. "I want a future for my children," he says, "but I worry about what is written in the book, about what is coming." When I ask whether he can believe in the book without believing in the apocalypse, he says, "A Muslim must adhere to each of Islam's Five Pillars: belief in Allah, in His Messenger, in His Book, the Day of Judgment, and your fate. I must surrender to my fate."

I stop asking about Europe.

Abed snaps a remark in Arabic. Abu Hassar answers in a long stream, which is only interrupted when Abed raises his hand to still him. "I am arguing that a secular state does more to protect Islam than a religious one." Before Abed can finish, Abu Hassar interrupts him again, as if concerned that he'll get some upper hand in their debate by extolling his points to me in English. They continue, becoming a bit breathless. Abed throws a finger at Abu Hassar. "He thinks there has never been a truly Islamic state."

Their disagreement eases into a more sustainable rhythm. They lean toward one another, as close as a couple wrapped in the same blanket. Outside, the cats continue their hunt for too few scraps of food. The children have finished their game of tag, and my eyes search the corners of the park for them but find no one. In the café the backgammon counters smack against the boards and the day's newspaper pages are spread across the tables. The old men play and argue with the brims of their hats pulled low, as if to hide their faces, leaning toward one another over their game boards. An old, tired calico with scars cut into his tufts of fur lopes across the park. Fearlessly, he leaps next to me in the booth. He stretches out, arching his back and extending his claws, which he then retracts as he tucks his paws under his soft belly. Shutting his eyes, he rests in a wide break of sunlight alongside my leg. I pet his back.

Abed, Abu Hassar, the old men—from them a new sound arises. All of their political arguments, their arguments about war, about religion, slowly blend together. And then, like a thousand discords ascending into a single keynote, they merge. The effect is ventriloquism, one strange voice without a source.

A SWISS WEDDING

NEUCHÂTEL

The snow from last winter still clings to certain peaks. Not necessarily the highest ones, but the cold peaks that face the wind and see less of the sun. The bare slate ridges below will remain exposed for a few weeks more. The valley is green, though autumn edges the leafed maples and oaks. Wired fences parcel neat geometries out of the farm country. Bovine herds chew their cud and drink from troughs of alpine melt drawn from Lake Neuchâtel. Everything slopes toward the lake: the peaks, the ridges, the fields, and the town of Bevaix, which clings to the banks. Tomorrow Abed and Laetitia will marry in its abbey, the Abbaye de Bevaix.

I arrive late, at around eight p.m., though the sun is still up. I eat dinner in the inn where I am staying. There is no one to bump into at the restaurant, no out-of-town guests. Laetitia's family and friends mostly live in the surrounding area—Lausanne and Geneva. The week before the wedding, Abed calls me to make sure I am still coming. When I assure him that I am, he asks if I will stand as his witness. Flattered, I accept, but then realize he has nobody else to ask. With his family trapped in Damascus, I represent the entirety of the groom's party.

Early the next afternoon, before the ceremony, I stroll along Bevaix's single-lane roads. I give myself enough time to get lost, and then do. An occasional car passes. In backyards hidden by hedgerows I hear children. The noise of my heel-strikes keeps me company through the disorienting stillness. I wander generally toward the lake until I see the stone redoubt of the abbey perched on a hilltop above the water. Its heavy walls seem to defend against a threat long since left, and its terraced fields, once tended by a congregation of monks, slope toward the banks of the lake. Pear trees line the abbey's walk. They have dropped their fruit, and the crushed pulp smells sweet. Bridesmaids, almost a dozen of them, tie a bouquet of balloons to a pair of steel knockers on the abbey's open oak door. In the back garden Laetitia and Abed take photos. He wears a dark suit, white shirt, and royal-blue tie. A red chiffon covers her shoulders, which arch forward, lithe as a question mark. While the photographer changes lenses, the two consider the lake, their arms looped around each other's waists. Then more pictures and the two turn their backs to the vista.

Harp music spills from the abbey's door. Abed and Laetitia pass through a side entrance, toward the nave. I wander in through the front, past the balloons, into a groin-vault arcade whose stone arches trap the cold. Fifty of us gather beneath the ample light of high dormer windows. The delicate hum of conversational French rises above the harp's notes. A young woman wearing a knee-length cocktail dress grabs my elbow, seemingly relieved to find me. "You are Elliot?" she asks, and then hurries me to a small corner room, where I find Abed and Laetitia sitting knee to knee. Abed stands and tells me I look good, and I tell him the same. Neither of us has seen the other so dressed up, and I notice the vent on his suit jacket is still sewn shut with an X of white thread from the factory. The four of us—the maid of honor, Laetitia, Abed, and then me—are organized in a line by another woman wearing a dour gray suit: a Swiss official, the justice of the peace.

The harp plays a processional. We walk past flickering candelabras toward an altar where the four of us stand, facing the official. She motions for us to sit and we perch rigidly on a single pew without a back. The civil ceremony begins in French, which Abed does not speak. Laetitia leans toward him, quietly whispering a translation. The official slows the ceremony, giving Laetitia time. As Abed struggles to understand his vows, he glances over to me now and again, plaintively, as if apologizing that I can't understand either.

That a former American Marine should serve as the sole witness to a new life embarked upon by a former Syrian activist feels appropriate. We are veterans of the same war, the same disillusionment, one where high-minded democratic ideals left a wake of destruction, forcing both of us to craft new lives from the ruins. Sitting next to my friend, the particulars of his vows seem less material than the choice he's made, to start again. What does it matter that we can't understand?

The Swiss official asks for the rings.

Abed points to my coat pocket. Then he holds Laetitia's hand and speaks to her in Arabic, offering his vow in a language they share. She does the same for him. The wedding party stands; so does everyone else. We walk over to a large registry, which the justice of the peace opens. While everyone trickles out of the abbey, we sign documents that make Laetitia and Abed husband and wife. They pose for a few final photos in front of the altar while I wander outside, to where the bridesmaids are handing out balloons from the bouquet they had tied to the abbey's door. They encourage each of us to write a wish on a slip of paper and to safety-pin that wish to our balloon's ribbon. Quickly our wedding party organizes into two ranks. The harp plays again from inside the abbey. When Laetitia and Abed emerge through the doors, we all release our balloons. Our heads are thrown backward. We cheer as the balloons find currents of air that will carry them over Lake Neuchâtel, toward the Alps, and perhaps even over the frozen peaks.

At the door of the abbey, Laetitia weaves her fingers through Abed's. While everyone's attention is fixed upward, his eyes stray toward a nearby copse of trees. He wanders away from Laetitia, away from the wedding party, to where an irregular gust has blown a few unfortunate balloons. Standing alone beneath the trees, he swats at the limbs overhead, struggling to free what has become ensnared in the branches.

BACK TO THE CITY

BAGHDAD, FALLUJAH, MOSUL

Three days I've been here, running from one ministry to another, making phone calls, emailing the US embassy, asking favors of friends, and then favors of friends of friends. Nothing has worked. I want to be in Fallujah. But I can't get out of Baghdad. It's two in the afternoon on a Thursday in late October. I'm in a nearly empty shopping mall, at a Toll House cookies kiosk across the street from the Iraqi Ministry of the Interior. It's Fityan, Hawre, and me. We're waiting for a call from Fityan's cousin Tahrir, who is a captain in the police. He is inside the ministry negotiating my letter of permission into Fallujah.

In Fallujah there is a doorway I want to stand in. Dan Malcom was shot and killed trying to cross its threshold as he stepped onto a rooftop twelve years ago. A sniper's bullet found its mark beneath his arm, just under the ribs.

In Fallujah there is a building I want to stand on top of. It was a candy store. The day after Dan was killed, my platoon fought a twelve-hour firefight from its rooftop. That was the worst day of the battle.

That doorway in Fallujah, that rooftop—I remember exactly where they are.

Fityan's phone rings, startling him so much that a worm of ash tumbles from his cigarette. He brushes at the black T-shirt that is snug over his round belly. As he answers Tahrir's call, I try to decode the jerky tonality of Fityan's Arabic. His expression sags as he hears his cousin's report.

"They are asking for a five-hundred-dollar bribe," Fityan says. He tosses his phone onto the coffee table between us. Fityan and Tahrir are Sunni, with deep ties in Iraq's restive al-Anbar Province. I met Fityan through Matt, who knew him through one of his students at the American University of Iraq in Sulaimani, which is to say he hardly knew Fityan at all. Weeks ago, over long-distance Skype calls and emails, Fityan introduced me to Tahrir. The two of them promised that they could get me into Fallujah, and I've come a long way because of their promises. "If you were Iranian, it'd be easier," Fityan mutters. "The ministries are all Shia. They're giving you a hard time because you're an American."

Our server brings us our drinks. Hawre, a photographer I've been working with, sets down his camera and examines the enormous cup of coffee in front of him. "Fityan, tell him I ordered a medium." Hawre is an Iraqi Kurd from Kirkuk, north of Baghdad. His teeth are crooked and overlapping, like a deck of cards fanned out by an unskilled dealer. Whenever he parts his lips, it looks like he's smiling. He is immensely proud that he hardly speaks Arabic.

Fityan confirms that Hawre's coffee is the size he ordered.

"Toll House is an American chain," I say to Hawre, attempting to explain his enormous "medium." Everyone lights cigarettes.

It's been twelve years since I was last in Fallujah. If a bribe is all that's preventing my return to the city, it seems I have no choice. "I could just pay the five hundred."

"They always do this bullshit," Fityan says.

They is Iraq's Shia-majority government, which has marginalized the country's Sunni minority since the United States officially withdrew in 2011. Shia flags emblazoned with the deific portrait of Ali—the Prophet Muhammad's martyred cousin and son-in-law—line nearly every government building, lamppost, and shop front in Baghdad. Ali has an impenetrable black beard, a confrontational stare, and a forest-green shroud covering his head. The Shia believe that he was Muhammad's legitimate successor, and he has become for them the personification of resistance to the Islamic State.

As I wait for Tahrir to return, I slump in my chair and sit for another hour. Dysfunction in this country is millennia deep. Why did I expect that Tahrir and Fityan, two Sunnis from al-Anbar, would be able to navigate the bureaucracy of an Iranian-backed Shia government?

Then Tahrir appears, strutting past the cashier, who, like everyone else, is nearly a head shorter than him. "Elliot, bro, you look sad. Why the long faces?"

I'm about to ask him if I should pay the bribe when from behind his back he whips forward a brown envelope closed with an official seal. Handwritten Arabic script is lashed along its front. I go to tear it open as if it were one of Willy Wonka's golden tickets. "Slow down," he tells me. He takes back the envelope and gently places it on the table.

"What about the bribe?" I ask.

"I was fucking with you, *habibi*. You Americans think we Iraqis can't do anything right," he says. "I told you, the guy at the ministry is my friend."

We carefully remove the letter, a single page covered with seals and serial numbers and many signatures. "What does it say?" I ask.

Fityan reads the text, his mouth silently forming the words in Arabic while the tip of his cigarette bounces over the syllables with metronomic precision. He glances up at me. "It says you're going back to Fallujah."

———

Early on Friday morning, the first day of the Muslim weekend, Baghdad is asleep as we drive out of the city's deserted streets. Fityan and Tahrir are up front, and Hawre's next to me in the back seat, hungover with a pair of knockoff Gucci sunglasses pulled over his eyes. He's leaning his head against the window when his phone rings. The voice on the other end is frantic, and soon Hawre is frantic as well. "No, no," he repeats. He tucks his phone away. "That was my brother. At four a.m. the Daesh attacked Kirkuk."

Four days ago, the Iraqis began an offensive to retake Mosul from the Islamic State. Thus far, an alliance of Iraqi security forces, Kurdish peshmerga, and Shia militias known as Hashd al-Shaabi, or Popular Mobilization Forces, has made steady advances toward Mosul. These gains come on the heels of more than a year's worth of successful offensives by Iraqi security forces in Tikrit, Hit, Rutbah, Ramadi, and Fallujah. Prime Minister Haider al-Abadi has staked the credibility of his government on the Mosul operation's success, appearing on television to announce the offensive in the black uniform of his elite counterterrorism forces.

The attack on Kirkuk was part of an Islamic State counteroffensive. We scroll through Facebook and Twitter, searching for news. "The Daesh are fucking smart," Tahrir says as we pull up to the last checkpoint on the outskirts of Baghdad. A sentry makes a long examination of my passport and letter from the interior ministry. Tahrir has worn his police uniform for good measure, an ad hoc mixture of camouflage pants and an olive-green safari shirt. His pistol is tucked into his waistband. Opposite us, the queue of vehicles entering Baghdad extends for nearly half a mile. The lane of traffic departing for al-Anbar is virtually empty. We are waved through.

The highway stretches out with palm groves on either side. More than a decade ago, on daylong foot patrols, our platoon would rest in the trees' shade with our backs to their scaled trunks and our rifle barrels facing outward. Soon Abu Ghraib, the infamous Iraqi prison, appears. The cupolas of its guard towers menace the prisoners inside and the travelers on the road: *Watch where you're going and what you do.* Villages with low-slung dwellings and names as forgettable as passwords race by: Nasir Wa Salam, Zaidan, Amiriyat. There are also the places we named ourselves, because we knew no better, like the bulging peninsula cut by the Euphrates that separates al-Anbar and Babylon. We called it the "ball sack."

After twelve years, everything is unchanged. And looming over it now, as it did then, is Fallujah. Fityan points up the road, where four- and five-story buildings form a barricade on the horizon. "There it is," he says. A picket of minarets stab heavenward, their sides paneled with crumbling mosaics. Everything anyone has ever built in this city is pocked with bullet holes. "Is it like you remembered it?" Fityan wants to know.

———

At a barbed-wire checkpoint decorated with flowers to welcome returning residents, we meet Colonel Mahmoud Jamad, the city's chief of
police, who escorts us to his headquarters. He is a member of the Albu
Issa tribe, which supported the al-Anbar Awakening, a Sunni movement that rebelled against al-Qaeda in Iraq. We are served bread, fried
eggs, and tea with a finger's worth of sugar lurking at the bottom. We
sit in his office, his unmade bed in the corner, a pair of his socks airing
out on the windowsill. A clicking table fan circulates the inside air.

For nearly an hour Colonel Jamad tells us how the city is being rebuilt, but what he says doesn't correspond with what we see. Though
Iraqi security forces retook Fallujah from the Islamic State four months
ago, in June, three-quarters of the city's population has yet to return.
There is still no electricity, no water, no sanitation. Colonel Jamad grew
up in Fallujah and has worked in and around the city as a police officer
since 2005—longer than anyone, he tells us. "I will never give up on my
home," he says. One can't begrudge him his persistence. In his job only
an optimist—even a foolish one—could hold out any hope for success.

"The Daesh are vampires," Colonel Jamad says. "I insist on this description. They suck the life from everything." He suggests that we visit
an Islamic State prison the Iraqi security forces discovered after liberat-
ing the city. I agree but also ask to visit a couple of other buildings, obscure ones. Before he has a chance to ask why, there is a commotion at
the front of the police station. A tall officer in a well-starched uniform
with deliriously embroidered epaulettes and a retinue in tow steps into
Colonel Jamad's office. It is Brigadier General Mahmoud al-Filahi, commander of the Iraqi Army's Tenth Division, which is responsible for all
of al-Anbar Province, here for an impromptu visit.

Colonel Jamad assigns us an escort of a few soldiers and ushers us hastily out of his office so that he can speak with the general alone. As I pack up my things, Colonel Jamad explains our plans to General al-Filahi. The general's questions are pointed. "And what is it that you're looking for?"

I hesitate, not certain that I want to offer up this detail. Before I can respond, the general adds, "Perhaps you are looking for your WMDs?"

I smile and laugh lightly at his joke. He does not.

"Life is like chess," Dan would sometimes say, usually when he was winning. We played our last game sitting across from each other with his magnetic set spread over an upturned crate of MREs. When he was killed on the five-story high-rise, he was sprinting across the flat rooftop toward a door that would have taken him downstairs to relative safety. He collapsed across the threshold, dying almost instantly, or so I was told. He's buried at Arlington now. I heard that his magnetic chessboard was in his cargo pocket when he was killed.

After we leave the police headquarters in Fallujah, Hawre wants to walk. So do I. But our two escorts shepherd us into the bed of a pickup truck instead. The mayor's complex is a few hundred meters away, on the north side of Highway 10, whose four lanes bisect the city. Across the street is the timeworn candy store, the other place I want to see. Tahrir begins to argue with our escorts in Arabic, insisting that they take us there. Fityan pulls me aside and says, "We're not telling them that you fought here, so they're a bit confused." I can't disagree with his judgment. Visiting this city as a former Marine feels like walking through New Orleans if your name is Hurricane Katrina.

The escorts drive us to the mayor's complex—or what is left of it. The Islamic State leveled most government buildings during their occupation. Our escorts warn us to be careful as we step through the rubble. The city has yet to be demined and booby traps are uncovered daily. Among fragments of cement, I stumble across a human hip bone. I also find the skeletal remains of Mary-Kate, from whose rooftop I had called Dan. Searching the horizon, I see only blue sky where the highrise once loomed. Mysteriously, not even the wreckage remains.

Tahrir glances at the rubble beneath his feet. "Is this where it was?" he asks.

"No," I say. "It was over there." I point at the empty patch of ground.

"The door, *habibi*?"

"I guess it's gone."

I quickly find the candy store, where insurgents surrounded my platoon the day after Dan was killed. That morning, at three o'clock, we had crossed Highway 10 in advance of a larger assault of nearly one thousand Marines that was scheduled for later that morning. I had never seen the candy store from the outside in daylight. "This is the place," I tell Hawre. He begins to shoot photos, which only increases the suspicions of our Iraqi escorts. They toss furtive glances in my direction and whisper among themselves. The sign affixed to the side of the structure is in English. It reads, "Moonlight Supermarket."

A rusted mesh fence, padlocked shut, encircles the building. I climb up the side. By the time I am on the rooftop, I am covered in familiar dust. I recognize not so much the building as the vantages it offers. The view from where we set in our machine guns so they could rake a long street. The approach where we waited desperately for an armored ambulance as one of the Marines, who'd been shot through the femoral artery, was bleeding to death. The southeastern corner where I crouched alongside my platoon sergeant, who in his early thirties seemed infinitely old and wise, seconds before he was shot in the head, only to miraculously survive. The spot in the basement where we placed bricks of C4 explosive when, surrounded as we were, our company commander ordered us to advance further into the city and we knew going out the front door would be suicide so we blew open a door of our own, understanding that a single miscalculation would cause the entire building to collapse on top of us.

I try to imagine this place differently, not as a battlefield but as a community of homes and businesses. Many of our most iconic cities— Rome, Istanbul, Athens—have a layered architectural aesthetic, each population having built on what its predecessors created. Fallujah is different. It is defined not by creation but rather by destruction.

My eyes cast out in specific directions, searching for hard-fought neighborhoods and alleyways, for unrepaired scars on the buildings. I am searching for the marks we left behind. I see them everywhere, commingled with the marks left by others. They have become the city, both battlefield and home.

———

Colonel Jamad is eager for us to see the torture house. We've driven into Fallujah's Jolan District, where townspeople strung up the burned bodies of four American Blackwater contractors from a bridge in March 2004, beginning the first battle for the city. On every street in Fallujah the prickly scent of cordite lingers in the air, but it is heaviest up here in Jolan. We follow Colonel Jamad into the courtyard of a mansion. In the foyer, light pours through several stained glass windows. Above us, a chandelier's crystal pendants tinkle in time with a soldier's footfalls in an upper bedroom. We enter an atrium. A winding staircase leads up to a second story beneath a domed roof painted purple, yellow, and pink. Resting on the tiled floor is a human femur.

"These were the mass holding cells," says Colonel Jamad, "and the offices for the Daesh courts." Hastily welded steel doors enclose salon-sized rooms, with bags of dates and almonds stashed in the corners. "This is all they fed the prisoners," he explains. On a single shelf rests a small library consisting mainly of religious texts, and two curious exceptions: a collection of letters by Nelson Mandela with a foreword by Barack Obama, and *The Short Stories of H. G. Wells.*

Colonel Jamad announces that it's time for us to go next door. Instead of walking outside, he crawls through a hole that Islamic State fighters sledgehammered into the wall so they could move between buildings without being detected by coalition aircraft. "This is the place they don't want you to see," Colonel Jamad says of this second house. A fire has ripped through the interior: heat has warped and melted air-conditioning units, glass, anything not made of stone or steel. An eerie silence possesses every room. Hardly anyone in our group speaks, and none of us hazards more than a whisper. There is only the rhythmic sound of our steps crunching against the charred wreckage—that and the smell, a cauterized scent sickly sweet with the undertones of death.

We climb a stairwell. A hand-cranked winch is fastened to the banister. A pulley is bolted to the ceiling. The steel wires hanging from it have loops just large enough to cuff a pair of human wrists. Car batteries are stacked in a corner, and next to them are bales of copper wire with the insulation stripped away, as well as a melted plastic chair. It seems gratuitous to ask what it's all for. On the second floor, the windows are covered. It is pitch-black. I turn on my iPhone's flashlight. Six steel cages are arrayed in two rows. A thin mat and a pillow cover the floor of each cell, and a padlock is notched jauntily onto every door. "Step inside," Colonel Jamad insists. I hesitate. He asks again, challenging me. I duck my head and walk into the solitary confinement cell. "Turn off your light," he says. I do, for maybe three seconds, possibly for as long as five—long enough, in any event, for him to tell me through the impenetrable darkness, "What you see are the accomplishments of the US government."

Spray-painted in white on an interior courtyard wall is the first part of the shahadah: *la ilaha illallah*, "There is no god but God." Heaped beneath the Islamic State graffiti are a handful of hair dryers and curling irons. Colonel Jamad dips his wrist effeminately and laughs. "The Daesh," he tells us, "are very vain, especially about their hair." He is still amused by this as we amble out into the bright street, squinting against the sunlight.

As we walk, the city's energy refreshes Colonel Jamad. He is eager for us to speak with the few locals. Sitting in front of a boarded-up shop is a stout man in a gray, ankle-length dishdasha and Nike sandals. He is passing a tangle of wire to his nephews, who are coiling it around a scrap of wood. "Wire is expensive, so we're digging up what's left in the city and using it in our homes," he explains.

The man's name is Ahmed Abas al-Jabor. He is a *mukhtar*, a local community leader. When I ask if he was here during the Islamic State's occupation, he insists that he was not. His nephews shift restlessly about and insist that they too left the city. Fityan, who has been translating, leans toward me. "No one is going to admit that they stayed," he whispers. Al-Jabor continues, "Many are waiting to see if the insurgents will retake the city."

Colonel Jamad cuts him off. "Don't call them insurgents."

Al-Jabor stares back at him blankly.

"You must call them Daesh."

Every tenth house or so, someone is trying to rebuild, clearing out a courtyard, sweeping up debris, tampering with a generator. True to Fityan's word, citizens across the board tell me they left Fallujah during the Islamic State occupation. Along intersections and street corners we see a smattering of Iraqi police and army checkpoints. Not all, but many, fly the Shia flags emblazoned with the image of Ali that were so ubiquitous around Baghdad. The destructive evidence of this summer's battle—and those that preceded it—is apparent everywhere.

We spend the afternoon outside of Fallujah, at Habbaniyah Air Base. Unbeknownst to us, Colonel Jamad has arranged a VIP visit to the Iraqi police's Special Tactical Regiment. The regiment's commander, Lieutenant Colonel Adel Hamed, tells us hair-raising stories about the recent battles for Ramadi and Fallujah, replete with slick promo videos made by his in-house media team. His men, trained by Navy SEALs, served as shock troops in both battles. When I ask the colonel how his background landed him a job as the leader of an elite commando unit—he once worked as an administrative officer—he shrugs and says that nobody else wanted the position. He tells us that he raised the Iraqi flag over Ramadi's city hall himself and then shows us a video to prove it. (At his urging, we watch it several times.) He is also eager to show off a picture of himself with a bandage over his left eye, sunglasses down. The photo shows him in Ramadi, strutting along a highway flanked by the skeletal wreckage of buildings, his men trailing behind him. Gesturing upward, presumably at the enemy, his hand is formed into a karate chop. "I took a grenade fragment in my eye," he says. "It's still there. And on that day, I realized my purpose in life: I love fighting more than anything else."

After a tour of his barracks, armory, and motor pool—the last of which is filled with bullet-riddled Humvees and the occasional ballistic windshield shattered by rifle fire—I find myself chatting with one of his troopers, a slim man who, despite his sunken chest and tobacco-stained teeth, strikes a debonair resemblance to Omar Sharif. He speaks perfect English and is the regiment's JTAC—joint tactical air controller—meaning he is qualified to call in air strikes from Western warplanes. He calls himself Maximus, a nod to Russell Crowe's character in *Gladiator*. It seems the SEALs' talents for self-promotion have rubbed off on their Iraqi counterparts. Maximus, one of the most well-trained troopers in this unit, is also his regiment's press liaison. He follows us around wearing a khaki safari vest with "Media Officer" embroidered on the chest.

"I used to work with the Marines," he tells me. "Three-seven, one-nine, two-eight—those are my boys." I tell him I was with "one-eight," otherwise known as the First Battalion of the Eighth Marine Regiment. "Right on, man," he says, his head nodding in a rhythmic groove. We chat a bit more about Fallujah, Ramadi, and our respective battles in these cities. When I offer my hand, he shakes it but then rotates his palm in mine and pulls me in for an American-style bro hug.

Soon we are back on the road, driving toward Fallujah. "What did you think?" Tahrir asks. Before I can answer, he continues, "They're as good as most Americans."

I can't disagree, but the conclusion is unsettling. With select units like the Special Tactical Regiment, the United States has managed to create a security apparatus built in its own image. These elite groups are well trained and well equipped and have won decisive battles against the Islamic State in Fallujah and Ramadi. They will do the same in Mosul. But winning battles was never the US military's problem. The problem was always what came after, the rebuilding.

As the afternoon sun descends, the rubbled outskirts of Fallujah come into view. We pull over by the Moonlight Supermarket so that Hawre can take a few more photographs before we return to Baghdad. Hawre wanders across the street, followed by Tahrir. The city's residents step from their homes and surround Tahrir. His uniform seems to confuse them. I imagine they have mistaken him for a member of the local police and are accosting him with questions about when, if ever, they can hope to see basic services return to their city.

While Fityan speaks to our Iraqi escort, I notice a broken cinderblock wall on the back side of the supermarket. It forms a corner, maybe three feet on one side and five on the other, and rises a little higher than my knees. I crouch behind it, into a familiar position. When our platoon escaped from the candy store twelve years ago, I found myself pinned behind this tiny wall for about twenty minutes as we struggled to advance deeper into Fallujah. A flood of memories returns. The clattering of tank treads. The panicked squelch of radio traffic. The terrified, uncomprehending looks of the Marines around me. How by that afternoon I had shouted myself hoarse, and was reduced to issuing orders under fire in a depleted whisper. I glance over the wall, toward the mayor's complex, to the void in the sky where the high-rise once stood, the place where Dan was killed. I reach over to the wall's far side. Under my hand, I can feel tiny gouges. My fingertips read them like braille. I wonder if they were made that day in 2004.

I occasionally still play chess. During a game with a Turkish friend at a café in Istanbul, I once reiterated Dan's words, explaining as I took a piece that life was like chess. My friend laughed at me. "No, it's not." He gestured toward another table, where players rolled dice from a cup across a board. "Life is backgammon. The game takes skill, but it also takes luck." As he said this, I thought about the bullet that found Dan. I often think about the bullet that never found me.

When I return to Fityan and our Iraqi escort by the car, they are silent for a moment, until the soldier asks what I was looking at.

I tell him that I've been here before. Then I explain about the candy store and the mayor's complex. He wants to know why I chose to come back.

"To see what it was like now, I guess."

He looks at me, perplexed. "It is just as you left it."

———

Two days later, Hawre and I are driving again. Fixed along the horizon is Bartella, on the outskirts of Mosul. The town is burning. Noxious columns of smoke lift upward, like stitches fastening earth to sky. Yesterday, Hawre and I left Baghdad and headed north to join the offensive. Now, around two p.m., our Toyota HiLux is stopped on the shoulder of the road, alongside a mélange of tanks, armored bulldozers, and black Humvees from the Iraqi Counter Terrorism Service's First Brigade, also known as the Golden Division. Bartella is a Christian town and the

Golden Division, with its Shia flags fluttering from the back of every other vehicle, will soon liberate it from more than two years of Islamic State occupation.

Soldiers in black uniforms and black ski masks escort a pair of priests into a white Suburban, and I find myself trying to remember when, in the history of war, there has been another instance where the good guys wore black uniforms and black ski masks. The priests plan to hold Mass that afternoon in the Church of Mart Shmoni, in the center of Bartella. As their Suburban pulls into the street, Hawre and I pull up behind them, but a soldier with the Golden Division cuts us off. I offer my press credentials—a dog-eared letter from *Esquire* magazine—and my passport. Hawre argues with him in Kurdish. He reaches into his pocket and hands the soldier his Iraqi identification card. "He wants to keep your passport until we come out of Bartella," Hawre says.

"I'm not giving him my passport."

"Then we can't go," Hawre says. A beat passes. "Don't worry," he pleads, "I've got his cell phone number."

The soldier grins. He's missing one of his incisors, and another tooth is made of gold. "I be here when you back," he tells me in choppy English. I hand him my passport and our HiLux slides behind the priests.

About a day after the Golden Division launched its assault on Bartella, we hear early estimates that eighty Islamic State fighters lie dead in the town. On either side of the road, scorched swaths of dry grass spot the ground. Nearly every building is a mass of twisted rebar and collapsed cinder blocks. Snaps of rifle fire and the low percussive thuds of artillery and air strikes can be heard in the distance, causing confused flocks of birds to leap from their perches and juke across the skyline. A sedan passes us going the opposite direction. Hunched behind its steering wheel, with his eyes barely above the dashboard, is a boy not much more than ten years old. Two little girls even younger than him are in the back seat. They are wearing school uniforms. We pass a road sign: "Mosul, 27 km."

Unlike Fallujah, which encompasses sixteen square kilometers, Mosul and its environs are sprawling. The battles for Fallujah in 2004 involved little maneuver. We cleared house-to-house through dense urban blocks. This battle feels different. Thus far, it has seen movement along multiple axes of advance. We are to the east of Mosul, with the Iraqi security forces. To the north and south is the Kurdish peshmerga, as well as other units of the Iraqi security forces. Waiting in reserve is the Iranian-backed Hashd al-Shaabi, whose presence is controversial. Prime Minister Abadi has promised that neither the Hashd al-Shaabi nor the peshmerga will participate in the fight for Mosul itself; that the final assault will be the work of the nominally secular Iraqi security forces, including the Golden Division. But if Islamic State resistance proves too much for the Iraqi security forces, the peshmerga and the Hashd al-Shaabi might very well find themselves immersed in the battle, further inflaming sectarian tensions along Shia, Sunni, and Kurdish lines. What will happen inside of Mosul is the question on everyone's mind.

A sergeant flags us down, instructing us to park. Hawre and I will have to travel the rest of the way on foot. Humvees and dismounted soldiers rush past us, setting up their positions in the newly liberated town. The soldiers' voices are jubilant. Several who fought this morning now strip to the waist and wash with bottled water. Others clean weapons. I meet a soldier who is working on the grenade launcher in his

Humvee's turret with a rag and oil, and ask him for directions to the church. He isn't certain, but he is eager to talk. He says that the Daesh "are good with ambushes and IEDs, but not as good in conventional battle." He explains that his family is proud of him: "I have been fighting nonstop for a year, but they don't worry. If I die, I will be a martyr." He insists that I take down his name: "Maher Rashid from Baghdad." I ask him again if he knows where the church is. Before he can answer, the bells toll, for the first time in two years. "That way," he says.

Affixed to the dome of the Church of Mart Shmoni are two tree limbs hastily lashed together into a cross. An Iraqi flag flies from its top. There is an enormous gouge in the side of the church in the shape of a crucifix, no doubt the work of the Islamic State. Inside, upturned pews litter the nave. The altar in the sanctuary is covered in rubble but still intact. The priests continue to toll the bells. Soldiers file in and out of the ravaged church. They take selfies next to destroyed artifacts. Not even the priests think to stop them.

Between here and Mosul, there are a dozen more Bartellas to clear. But for today, the Golden Division's work is done. The discipline they maintained for the battle ebbs away, devolving into horseplay. They take off their boots and body armor and walk around in flip-flops and T-shirts. A grinning artillery gunner wears a T-shirt with a skull that reads "*KILL 'EM ALL, Let God Sort 'Em Out!*" Another soldier has chosen a tank top with a spray-brushed portrait of a lion staring into the sunset. A burly sergeant is attempting to throw his bayonet as close as possible to his opponent's foot, in a makeshift game of mumblety-peg.

I feel a tap on my shoulder. A soldier stands behind me, cradling a ceramic statue of the Virgin Mary. I take his picture, which seems to satisfy him. Then a lanky, baby-faced private wanders up and panto-mimes slashing the blade of his bayonet across his own neck. His eyes go wide, and with a broad, homicidal grin he says, "Daaaeeeeesh." His buddies laugh. The sergeant wanders over. He explains that tomorrow they'll continue their advance at first light. They plan to liberate three more villages, he says, before muttering under his breath, "*Inshallah.*"

I am anxious to retrieve my passport, so I find Hawre. We wander back toward our HiLux. Ahead of us is a consistent rumble of artillery and air strikes. Behind us we can hear the chatter of the Golden Division as it beds down for the night. The soldiers' voices are cheerful, confident of victory. From behind a flatbed ammunition truck parked in a field, someone calls out to me. When I turn, a hulking figure wearing an old, American-style desert uniform with a brown T-shirt comes jogging forward with a broad smile, his enormous gut swaying in rhythm with his steps. "Cigarette, *habibi*?" I reach into my coat pocket and offer him a Marlboro Light. "Oh, no, I don't like Lights. You American?" he asks, taking out one of his own cigarettes, a brand called Pine. "My sister, she lives in America, in Texas."

"Oh yeah, where in Texas?" My mother is from Texas.

He glances back at me, confused. "In Texas!"

"No, what part—Dallas, Houston?"

"Like I say, in Texas."

His name, he says, is Firaz Saleh Mohammad. I take it down at first just to be polite. He is a sergeant. Then he explains how he helped his sister immigrate because "I've been a soldier longer than anyone. I was ICDC, *habibi*," he says, referring to the Iraqi Civil Defense Corps, the precursor to the Iraqi Army that was founded in 2003 and summarily dissolved a year later. "I have been here since the very beginning, starting with the ICDC and Marines in Fallujah in 2004. No one has seen as much as I have seen."

I tell him that I was in Fallujah in 2004.

"I was with one-five. You know one-five?"

"Yes, I know one-five." A few friends come to mind. "I was with one-eight."

He puts his arm around me and laughs. "What are you doing here?" he asks. "Did you get lost?" I don't say anything, and he doesn't push it. He just smiles, jabs his finger in my face, and repeats, "My sister, she is very happy in Texas." As he finishes his cigarette, he's looking to the west, toward Mosul.

"What do you think's going to happen?" I ask him.

He shakes his head. "This? The future of all this, it cannot be predicted."

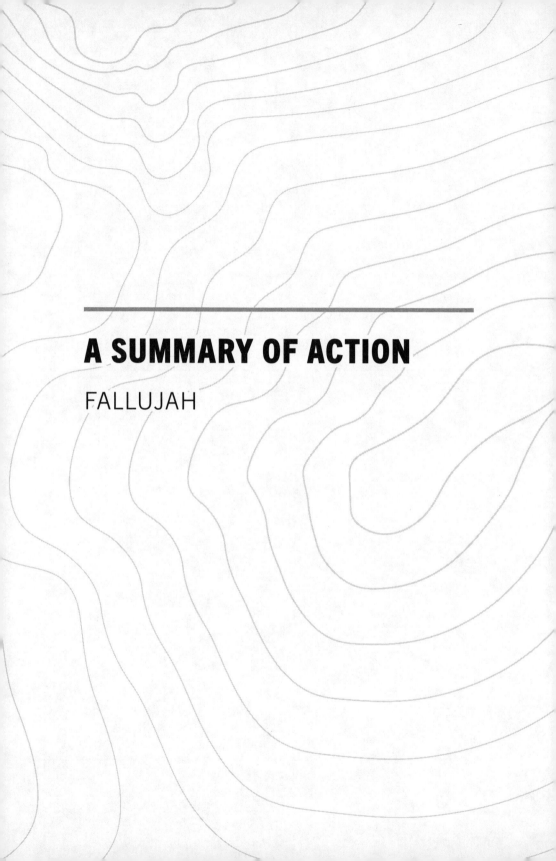

A SUMMARY OF ACTION

FALLUJAH

Two years after the Battle of Fallujah, on a clear January day in Camp Lejeune, I was awarded a medal. My entire family came for the occasion. It was my last day in the battalion, which was standing in formation on the parade ground while the adjutant for the Second Marine Division read a citation. Most of the Marines I'd fought alongside weren't there—two years is a long time in the Corps, so they'd moved on, to civilian life, to other postings—but a few stood in formation. I searched for their faces, but I'd lost them in the ranks. After the award was presented, I was handed the citation and the more detailed "summary of action." Mine was written by my company commander. It is the story of what happened. Rereading it now, all these years later, I want to add some things—the kinds of things that don't make it into formal government documents, the personal reflections that fill the lines between them.

———

During this period of time, SNO (... *Said Named Officer* ...) received imminent danger pay. (... *when we came back most of us didn't know what to do with all the imminent danger pay we'd saved up. We spent it on cars, on motorcycles, or partying. I spent some of mine on a weeklong trip running with the bulls in Pamplona . . .)*

Lieutenant Ackerman is enthusiastically recommended for the Silver Star for his heroic actions during OPERATION PHANTOM FURY in Fallujah, Iraq, between 10 November and 10 December 2004. *(. . . we wrote awards during the last days of the battle, when each officer—three of the remaining five lieutenants in my company— took turns working on a laptop fueled by a handheld diesel generator, while the next morning we'd once again be fighting . . .)* Lieutenant Ackerman's heroic actions during this period reflect a level of bravery, composure under fire, and combat leadership that is beyond expectations.

Lieutenant Ackerman served as a rifle platoon commander during OPERATION PHANTOM FURY. His platoon fought in more engagements than any other rifle platoon in the company. *(. . . two weeks into the battle, my company commander told me that I was both the luckiest and unluckiest lieutenant he'd ever met. The luckiest because right out the gate, I experienced the largest battle the Marine Corps had fought in decades. I was the unluckiest because everything I ever did after that would seem inconsequential . . .)* On numerous occasions he was tasked as the company's main effort during the company's attack south. During the course of the fighting in Fallujah, his platoon took casualties without the slightest degradation of motivation, professionalism, or effectiveness. *(. . . "I can't take it anymore," one of the Marines tells me. We're four days into the battle. His squad leader said he needed to talk to me. "I keep thinking about my daughter. Every time I go into a house I think about her."* He is crying and the other Marines are watching and I know that fear is contagious. "Do you want me to get you out of here?" I ask. He keeps muttering that he can't take it. Twenty minutes later I'm loading him into an amtrack that will drive him out of Fallujah alongside wounded Marines. He and Pratt are married to a set of sisters. Pratt says he'll never speak to him again...) Lieutenant Ackerman led his platoon with a level of disciplined violence that crushed the enemy and was critical to the company's success. (... on the back of an M1 Abrams tank there is a little telephone in a box, tapped into the crew's intercom; it's called a "grunt phone." I've never been as scared as I was the times I had to run to that grunt phone, bullet impacts dancing on the tank's armor, their ricochets flashing like fistfuls of thrown pennies. I needed to get on the grunt phone to tell the tanks where to shoot. The tank crew would listen to music on their intercom, so if no one was talking you'd hear pop songs when you held the handset to your ear. The tankers I worked with liked Britney Spears. The squat crew chief, who looked like he was born to fit inside of a tank, told me that he played the music because it helped everyone in the tank stay "frosty"...)

At 0400 on 10 November, the company crossed the line of departure on the north side of Fallujah and attacked to seize the government complex in the heart of the city. Lieutenant Ackerman was tasked with seizing the western side of the complex. (... it was the Corps' birthday. As we loaded the tracks, the Marines swapped little pieces of MRE cake and placed them gently in their mouths, like priests placing Communion wafers...) As the company made the initial breach into the compound, Lieutenant Ackerman

215

quickly established a foothold and seized the police station and high-rise building with little resistance. (... *Staff Sergeant Ricardo Sebastian, who we called Seabass, thought the insurgents might not fight, that they might withdraw. He was Dan's platoon sergeant. After my platoon sergeant was shot in the head, he became mine, but for less than two days, as he'd soon be shot through the arm and the leg. When we entered the mayor's complex and nobody was there, I thought maybe Seabass had been right...*) Using a combination of precise rocket shots and explosive breaches, he was able to quickly advance and clear his first two buildings prior to sunrise. (... *in the week before the battle, we'd rehearsed this dozens of times. We rehearsed and rehearsed and rehearsed as if rehearsing it enough meant we might never have to do it...*) As the sun came over the horizon, a heavy volume of enemy direct and indirect fire shattered the early-morning calm. It quickly became apparent that while there were no enemy personnel inside the compound, the buildings to the south, east, and west were teeming with insurgents. (... *Dan's up on the rooftop of the high-rise...*)

Lieutenant Ackerman quickly grasped the situation, and as the company began to respond to the enemy fire from all directions, he attacked and seized the southern-most buildings in the government complex. (... *we run as fast as we can to Mary-Kate and Ashley, kicking open locked doors, breaking windows; it is exciting, no one's been hurt, we are euphoric...*) From this position, he was able to provide timely and accurate reporting to the company commander on the enemy disposition that helped shape the company battle for the rest of the afternoon. From his position as the battalion's lead southern trace, Lieutenant Ackerman orchestrated both direct and indirect fires for six hours. (*...I am on my stomach, and each time I peek my head above the wall, I am convinced it's going to get shot off. Second Platoon is in the building next to ours. A friendly air strike accidently hits them. We hear them screaming on the radio as they call in their wounded, and it mixes with the sounds of our jets overhead...*) During this time he acted as a forward observer for numerous mortar and artillery missions and is credited with destroying 20 enemy personnel. (*...the most difficult thing in a firefight is to find the people you are shooting at. Someone will manage a glimpse of a muzzle flash, or a silhouette in a window, and we will all shoot in that direction. Then another glimpse, and again we all shoot. I call in artillery, mortars. A sniper sets up in a minaret, his single shots inching closer to us. We are cleared to call in an air strike. The tip of the minaret explodes. The Marines film it, cheering. Later, one of them downloads the video clip to my computer. I still have it. I know I should delete it, but I don't...*)

Under the cover of darkness in the early-morning hours of 11 November, Lieutenant Ackerman's platoon was tasked to attack to gain a foothold on the south side of MSR Michigan in order to open the MSR as an east-west line of communication. (*...no one has slept, and we won't really sleep for another two days. We are also running low on food and water. I catch the Marines stealing glances at me as I talk on the radio. They will do this constantly in the days and weeks to follow. They know that what is said over the radio—an order, a mission—can get them killed, but they have little control over these deci-*

sions. *When we come home, one of the Marines in our platoon has to see the base psych, or "wizard," for PTSD symptoms. When I tell him I understand what he went through, he tells me that I don't. He says, "If you had to drive at a hundred fifty miles per hour down the freeway, what's scarier— driving the car or riding shotgun?" . . .)* He quickly seized a building with minimal resistance and once again became the forward southern trace for the battalion. *(. . . we shot a few rounds from a gunship—a cargo plane with a 120 mm cannon—into the first building we had wanted to fight from. It collapsed. So we had to go even deeper into the city, probably too deep. I've always wondered if we should have turned back . . .)* As the sun came up on 11 November, his platoon was in a position to engage multiple formations of enemy personnel moving into positions to attack the government complex. *(. . . we occupied a candy store. We ate Pringles and chugged soda. We reinforced our windows with bags of salt, using them like sandbags. When we saw the first insurgents we couldn't believe how casually they were walking around. They didn't expect us that far into the city. When we killed them it felt like murder . . .)* The enemy quickly realized that Lieutenant Ackerman's position had to be destroyed in order for them to maneuver on the government complex. *(. . . the Marines are running room to room, shooting into the street. Above the window where one of our machine guns is peeking outside, there is a poster of a lake encircled by snowcapped mountains. I am looking at the poster when three men in black tracksuits bolt into the open. I don't see them until they are dead in front of us. One of them is lying on his side, with his head resting on the curb like it's a pillow. The machine gunner, a kid named Benji, looks back at me smiling . . .)* During the course of this firefight, his platoon took two casualties, to include his platoon sergeant, who was shot in the head but survived. (... *back in Lejeune, when he leaves our platoon, we give him his helmet as a gift. The other Marine, a nineteen-year-old named Brown, is shot through the femoral artery. We slip and fall on his blood. So we cut open a few bags of the salt and throw it on the ground. It takes a long time for the medevac to come. We're crawling across the room, trying to find the sniper who shot Brown, the salt and the blood crunching beneath our hands and knees...*) On two occasions, he exposed himself to enemy direct fire in order to pull the wounded Marines to safety. The first AAV that was sent for medical evacuation was hit with an RPG and engulfed in flames. (... *when I hear this on the radio, I don't tell anyone. Brown's pulse is fading...*) The second AAV had trouble finding the platoon casualty collection point due to the heavy enemy fire, smoke, and confusion. Lieutenant Ackerman, sensing the situation and recognizing the need to expedite the linkup, rushed into the street to flag down the AAV. (... *Banotai and I are out in the street. We're tossing smoke grenades everywhere, green smoke, purple smoke, yellow smoke, which marks our position, but we're also hidden in it. You can hear the bullet snaps from inside this cloud as they shoot at us, hoping for a lucky hit. I've often imagined what it looked like to them—just a huge burst of color that they're shooting at, hoping to kill whatever's inside. Then the Humvees show up. On the field hospital's operating table, Brown is given his last rites by the chaplain...*) He ran through a gauntlet of enemy fire to ensure his wounded Marines were evacuated. As soon as the linkup was complete, Lieutenant Ackerman bounded back to his building to resume the fight. *(... Brown survives. By this point, we're surrounded ...)*

As the battle raged around him, the company commander pushed him a section of tanks to help break the enemy attack. *(... we chase two tanks down the road. Some telephone wires tangle on the back tank's turret. The tank yanks the telephone poles from the ground and drags them along the street behind it like so many tin cans tied to a newlywed's car. The tank's main cannon takes off the sides of buildings ...)* Due to the volume of enemy fire, he ordered his Marines to pull off the exposed roof and find firing positions from inside the building. *(... an RPG slams into the roof, peppering us with shrapnel. It makes no sense for everyone to be up here ...)* He quickly recognized that he could not mark targets for the tanks from inside the building. As the Marines pulled off the roof, Lieutenant Ackerman ordered the machine gunners off the roof, grabbed their M240G, and began systematically marking targets for the tanks to engage with their main gun rounds. *(... "Benji," I say, "give me that." I snatch the machine gun from him and fire a burst for the tanks to see. The arc of my tracers goes clumsily high. "Jesus, give it back, sir," says Benji. His rounds are on target. The two of us stay up there and do it together ...)* He remained in this exposed position for over one hour and destroyed upward of 30 enemy. While marking targets for the tanks he simultaneously called for and adjusted indirect fires to within 90 meters of his position, with devastating effect on the enemy. *(... while I'm on the roof, our company executive officer finds our platoon. He rushes inside and asks, "Who's in charge!" Wounded Marines*

are scattered all over the ground floor. Someone weakly says, "Doc is,"
pointing to our nineteen-year-old corpsman. When I'm on the roof, I don't
want to come downstairs and see this. You are responsible for everything
your platoon does or fails to do. Responsible for everything . . .)

At 1430 on 11 November the company was given the task to
continue the attack to a phase line approximately 300 meters to the south of MSR Michigan. As he prepared his platoon for the push south, he was essentially isolated by
fire inside the house he occupied. *(. . . I stick my head out of the*
door and a machine gun's burst nearly takes it off . . .) An enemy RPK
gunner had a primary direction of fire across the only exit
point of his house. *(. . . on the alley's far side there is a wall, which a*
pair of pigeons are trying to land on. Every few seconds there is another
burst from the machine gun. The pigeons can't land and we can't get out
this way . . .) Lieutenant Ackerman made the decision to create
a breach in the very house he occupied. *(. . . coming back into*
the house, I see Banotai, and I say, "We're trapped. It's suicide if we go that
way." Later, Banotai tells me that when I said that, it was the most scared
he'd even been . . .) As the engineers conducted a breach to exit
the house, he had the machine gunners suppress while the
platoon exited the building and conducted a foot-mobile
linkup with the company and began the attack south. *(. . . there*
was so much dust, I thought the house might collapse before we could get
out of it . . .)

The company attacked south along two parallel alleys.
(. . . we were stuck on the street, banging our rifle butts against the

padlocked doors, trying to get inside . . .) Lieutenant Ackerman was tasked to attack down the eastern alley. He had two tanks in support of his platoon. After traveling only 30 meters down the alley, his platoon came under withering small-arms, machine-gun, and RPG fire from all sides. (. . . they shot down at us from the rooftops. I am crouching in a doorway, and Ames is next to me with his radio and its damn ten-foot antenna. It's so loud, the air itself is ringing, and I am soundlessly shouting into the radio, as if the incredible noise has devoured my voice. Little tufts of earth erupt near my feet as bullets impact all around . . .) Lieutenant Ackerman attacked with ferocity for three hours and essentially broke the back of what turned out to be the heart of the enemy defense in the battalion's sector. (. . . two Marines drag Banotai toward an amtrack. He's been knocked unconscious . . .) His aggressive use of tanks in the narrow alley combined with his penchant for leading from the front turned a potentially disastrous situation into a crushing blow against the enemy. (. . . an RPG explodes next to another Marine, shredding his pants. His legs are covered in blood, and from the waist down he's naked . . .) Lieutenant Ackerman never wavered during the fight, even after taking thirteen casualties. (. . . our platoon sergeant, two out of our three squad leaders, four out of our six team leaders—they are all evacuated. My socks are wet. I've once again sweat through my clothes . . .) He simultaneously directed tank fires, conducted critical coordination with his adjacent platoon, coordinated four separate medical evacuations, and continued to attack directly into the heart of the enemy with bulldog tenacity. He selflessly exposed himself to enemy fire to mark targets, direct tank fires, and adjust indirect fires on numerous occasions. His ability to project confidence and maintain a cool head under withering enemy fire was critical as his platoon took numerous casualties and faced a determined enemy. *(... I finally get a head count. About half of the platoon is gone ...)* As darkness fell, the company went firm in a row of houses at their assigned phase line and began preparing for the expected order to continue attacking south. *(... someone offers me a cigarette. It's the first one I've smoked since I was seventeen ...)*

At 2330 on 11 November, the company attacked south to the next battalion phase line. Lieutenant Ackerman's platoon reached their objectives on the assigned phase line under the cover of darkness with minimal enemy resistance. *(... one of our sister platoons fends off an attack. They fight all morning and into the afternoon. We find a torture house—hooks from the ceiling, steel cages, car batteries—much like the one I'll visit years later with Colonel Jamad. We wander through it while spending the rest of the day in reserve ...)* Despite the mental and physical fatigue he and his men were experiencing, Lieutenant Ackerman ensured his Marines were resupplied, briefed, and in a strong security posture. His ability to instill motivation among his men set the stage for the next day's fighting. *(... I once read an account by a German officer in the First World War who said that after each assault through the trenches, he would make sure to have his men eat afterward; that way they knew they were alive. I try to make sure everyone is eating ...)*

223

As the sun came up on 12 November, the company was once again subject to small-arms, sniper, and RPG fire. During the course of the day, he directed precision direct fires and indirect fires on a shadowy enemy that had quickly learned not to show themselves to the Marines. (*. . . we had also learned not to show ourselves to them. Instead we stand back, try to figure out where they are, and then fight from a distance . . .*) At 1900 on the night of 12 November, the company pushed to the next battalion phase line and went firm in a row of houses just north of an open field. (*. . . for the first time, we sleep a few hours, in shifts . . .*) As the sun came up on 13 November, the company again attacked south to the next battalion phase line.

As Lieutenant Ackerman's platoon occupied a house along the phase line, they came under intense small-arms, sniper, machine-gun, and RPG fire. (*. . . my first platoon sergeant has been replaced by Seabass. He's behind a low wall rimming the roof. I'm next to him. He's searching for a sniper with his scope. His rifle gets shot out of his hands. We duck down. When he picks up his rifle, the scope is shattered. The round had nicked its front and then passed over his left shoulder and right between us, just missing our heads . . .*) Throughout the day the enemy repeatedly attacked his position. As the company had been tasked to hold along the phase line, Lieutenant Ackerman used the opportunity to let the enemy expose themselves and be cut down by his fires as they attacked. During the course of the day, he destroyed numerous enemy personnel by adjusting indirect fires and employing accurate direct fires. (*. . . I sit on the roof with the radio. The sky is very blue. I'm so* *tired that I struggle to stay awake as I feel the sun on my face . . .)* He rallied his Marines for a daylong gunfight by moving from position to position and pointing out targets, instilling motivation, and leading by example.

During the day, Lieutenant Ackerman recommended to his company commander that if he pushed south approximately 150 meters, he would essentially be in an ambush position as the sun rose the following day. Under the cover of darkness on the early morning of 14 November, his platoon quietly moved 150 meters forward of the company position and set up a strong point with good fields of fire. *(. . . we snuck forward of the lines at around two a.m., the idea being that we'd set up like we did at the candy store. When I explained it to the platoon nobody said anything. The last time we did this, we wound up surrounded . . .)* As the sun came up his intuition paid off. As soon as it was light enough to see, a group of 25 enemy personnel were seen trying to get into a flank position to attack the company. *(. . . they were just standing at a bend in the road. They were all wearing black. I took my time calling in the mortars, but because they were at a bend in the road, I knew exactly where they were. I whispered the grid coordinates into the radio and then I waited . . .)* He expertly called for and adjusted indirect fires and engaged with direct fires to devastating effect. *(. . . they just disappeared when the rounds impacted. After a couple of minutes a gentle breeze cleared up the smoke. It looked like someone had dumped a pile of wet black rags in the road . . .)* As this initial firefight was happening, ISR assets reported multiple enemy formations moving toward his position. Over the next two hours he called for and adjusted approximately 250 81 mm mortar rounds and provided targeting direction for multiple close air support missions. The majority of the indirect fires were expertly adjusted to within 100 meters of his position. In addition to orchestrating the indirect and his organic direct fires, he was pushed a section of tanks that he used to devastating effect. From his exposed position on the roof, he worked the tank section like an extension of himself, directing main gun and heavy-caliber rounds into the enemy formations and positions from as close as 20 meters. The enemy continued to try and close with and flank his position and was repeatedly cut down by his fires. (... *when I come home, more often than you might expect, a stranger will ask me if I ever killed anyone ...*) His actions that morning dealt a tremendous blow to the enemy in both the sheer number of enemy personnel killed as well as demonstrating to them that massing for an attack would prove deadly. (... *for a long time, I didn't know how to answer that question. A friend of mine took to saying, "If I did, you paid me to," which eventually I also took to saying, but the first person who asks me is my cousin, and she is six years old ...*)

At 1300 on 14 November, the company was once again ordered to continue the attack south to the next battalion phase line. Lieutenant Ackerman's platoon was the company's western flank and was adjacent to a company from Third Battalion, First Marines. As he attacked south he systematically attacked to clear for 350 meters of dense, urban terrain. (... *we would come up to a house, and the Marines would kick the door in and then toss a grenade inside...)* In addition to coordinating his platoon in the attack, he had the situational awareness to coordinate with the unit on his western flank to ensure both units could maximize fires and mutually support each other. *(... if someone started shooting at us from the house, we'd learned to back off and call up a tank or a D9 armored bulldozer to level the walls instead of sending more Marines inside...)* During the attack south, his platoon came across numerous pockets of enemy resistance that had to be deliberately cleared with a combination of tank and infantry attacks. *(... but they soon learned that this is what we'd do. So they'd put a machine gun in the corner and two people hiding by the door. When the first Marine came inside, they'd stitch him up with the machine gun, and when he fell the two guys by the door would drag him inside. Is that Marine alive? Is he dead? You don't know, and now you have to go into that house and clear room-to-room...)* As his platoon reached the battalion phase line, he attacked to clear a building to serve as a strong point.

Once his building was secure and he was setting up security, he came under heavy fire from the houses directly adjacent to the one he occupied. *(... we are on the roof, setting in our security, when they start shooting at us from next door...)* As his platoon was the first one to reach the phase line, he had a responsibility to ensure the adjacent houses were cleared for the arrival of the remainder of the company. Due to the geometry of fires, he was unable to use tanks to assist in clearing the enemy-occupied buildings. (... *Seabass takes a shoulder-fired rocket and shoots it through the opposite window, but we are so close that it doesn't arm and so skids without exploding into their house...*) He planned and launched a fierce attack into the buildings using a combination of satchel charges, machine guns, grenades, and small arms. (... *Seabass leads six Marines downstairs. He's going to clear out the house next door while the rest of us keep fighting from the rooftop, hoping to keep the insurgents' heads down while Seabass presses the assault...*) The battle space for this fight consisted of front yards and courtyards. It was so constricted that the two elements were literally throwing grenades at each other from over the courtyard wall. Recognizing that the buildings had to be cleared prior to the advancing company's rapid arrival, he took the situation into his own hands. Lieutenant Ackerman led a handful of Marines in a final attack to clear the buildings. (... *I'm calling for Seabass over the radio, but he isn't answering. I don't know what's going on next door, so I run downstairs and into the other house. The ground floor is on fire. Langrebe, one of the younger Marines, a twenty-year-old lance corporal, has been shot through both legs, and he's dragging himself toward the front door. A can of gasoline sits in a corner and someone has lit a bunch of blankets and mattresses on fire, as if the insurgents want to burn down the house with themselves and us inside. I'm coughing on the smoke. I find Seabass in the corner...*) Throwing hand grenades and firing pistols at point-blank range, his small band of warriors went toe to toe with the determined enemy. During the close-quarters fight, Lieutenant Ackerman was wounded after taking shrapnel to his back. Two Marines from his team were also wounded. (... *the medevac shows up, and we're trying to load Langrebe and Seabass in the back. Seabass is loopy, hopped up on morphine and adrenaline, and he is shouting, "I'll be back, LT. I'll be back," as the doors to the amtrack slowly close. A silhouette on the rooftop leans out into the street. He flings a grenade, aiming for the open top hatch of the amtrack. The grenade sails through the air. I lose it in the sun. Then it hits the edge of the amtrack and bounces into the street right next to me. I run in the opposite direction, getting maybe three or four steps away, and I wince and feel its fragments hit me in the back right beneath my body armor ...*) Lieutenant Ackerman never wavered and his team did not stop until the enemy was killed and the houses secure. One of his Marines was shot in the ankle and wrist while in the process of throwing a grenade. With the pin already pulled, the Marine quickly regained his composure and put the grenade on target as a wounded Lieutenant Ackerman supported with point-blank pistol fires. (... *back inside, we're lobbing grenades around the corners, there's dust everywhere, I unload my pistol into the next room because I'm too scared to step into it with my rifle. I can hear them inside, speaking in gasps, shuffling through the debris, as slowly—grenade by grenade and bullet by bullet—we kill them ...*) His contagious combat leadership and ability to instill this type of dedication is the stuff of legends. The houses were declared cleared, and Lieutenant Ackerman coordinated a medical evacuation for his wounded Marines while he performed self-aid on himself and set his platoon into a strongpoint security position for future operations. (... *for the next few weeks little pieces of steel work their way out of my skin. Our platoon corpsman, who still has acne, picks them out for me at night like he's popping pimples . . .)*

On the morning of 15 November, the company pushed the final 400 meters to the regimental limit of advance, which was where the south side of the city met the open desert. Lieutenant Ackerman had successfully led his platoon through house-to-house combat covering three and one-half kilometers of built-up urban terrain. Upon reaching the limit of advance, his platoon was set into the company firm base, and he prepared to conduct detailed clearing operations in the assigned company sector. *(. . . in our rush to get through the city, we'd bypassed hundreds of fighters. When we got to the end, all of the Marines kept asking whether we would have to turn around to go back and reclear everything we'd been through, which we did . . .)*

Over the course of the next two weeks, his platoon would conduct detailed clearing operations in his assigned sector. This particularly dangerous task consisted of entering every house to destroy remaining enemy and reducing numerous caches. On multiple occasions, his platoon entered houses only to be met with intense small-arms fire and grenades. *(. . . I've been asked what was the most courageous thing I saw someone do during the battle. It was what nearly every Marine did during those weeks of going house to house, never knowing what was waiting behind each closed door, a month-long game of Russian roulette . . .)* Each time, he expertly isolated the house, then called in tanks, AAVs, or D9 bulldozers to physically reduce the house with fires or blades prior to entering. He helped perfect this emerging tactic that allowed a determined and suicidal enemy to be destroyed without throwing Marines into the house as fodder. *(... the battalion opposite ours decided after a few days that no Marine's life was worth a house, so their commander stopped ordering his Marines to clear out buildings. Instead, they bulldozed their entire sector ...)*

Over the course of the battle for Fallujah, Lieutenant Ackerman performed heroically. The example he set with his combat endurance, leadership, and aggressiveness is the standard that instructors at The Basic School and Infantry Officers Course strive to impress upon their students. His Marines follow him with a sense of awe and are truly inspired by his leadership. Lieutenant Ackerman is enthusiastically recommended for the Silver Star.

———

After a month in Fallujah, we are taken out of the city and to a base where we get a hot meal, a shower, and fresh uniforms. When I take mine off, there are holes in the back and bloodstains there as well as on the shoulders and the knees. Some guys throw their old uniforms away.

I can't.

I tie mine up in a plastic bag and put it in my pack. Two months later, when our tour is up, I worry that some customs officer at the airport might confiscate the uniform, declaring it a sanitary hazard. But that doesn't happen.

When I get home, I put it in my basement, hidden, where it has sat for the last fifteen years. My medals, I imagine, I will someday give to my daughter. The watch I wore in the war and still wear now I plan to give to my son. But this uniform—who is it for?

Sometimes I think about throwing it out. I don't need it.

Sometimes I think that maybe I should still keep it, but just wash it instead. What would it be like to see it clean?

But I haven't done that either.

So it just sits there. And from time to time, I take it out, look at it, press my fingers in the holes, trace out the blotchy stains, and wonder what's to be done with it, that bundle of clothes that, despite all the memories, is nothing more than an old, bloody, and tattered rag.

What sit we then projecting peace and war?
War hath determined us. . . .

—*Paradise Lost*, Book II
John Milton

Acknowledgments

My gratitude to the editorial staffs at *Esquire*, *The New Yorker*, *The New Republic*, *The Atlantic*, and *The Daily Beast*, with particular thanks to Lucas Wittmann, Nicholas Thompson, Chloe Schama, Bobby Baird, Michael Hainey, and Jay Fielden, all of whom believed in the many stories that make up this one story. To Scott Moyers, who encouraged me to take the writing deeper; the part of the book I'm the most proud of would not exist if it weren't for you. To PJ Mark, who has not only been there since the beginning but who was the beginning. To my mother, father, and brother, for giving me a place to come home to. To my children for giving me a reason to come home. And to Lea Carpenter, Chui, who told me to write it.